JINCHALO

For my grandfather.

Entire contents © copyright 2012 Matthew Forsythe.

Drawn & Quarterly
Post Office Box 48056 Montreal, Quebec Canada H2V 4S8
www.drawnandquarterly.com

First edition: February 2012 Printed in Canada
10 9 8 7 6 5 4 3 2 1

Library and Archives Canada Cataloguing in Publication
Forsythe, Matthew, 1976 –
Jinchalo / Matthew Forsythe
ISBN 978-1-77046-067-6
I. Title. PN6733 F67155 2011   741.5'971   C2011-905295-4

Drawn & Quarterly acknowledges the financial
support of the Government of Canada through the
Canada Book Fund and the Canada Council for the Arts
for our publishing activities
and for support of this edition.

Distributed in the USA by:
Farrar, Straus and Giroux
18 West 18th Street
New York, NY 10011
Orders: 888.330.8477

Distributed in Canada by:
Raincoast Books
2440 Viking Way
Richmond, BC V6V 1N2
Orders: 800.663.5714

JINCHALO

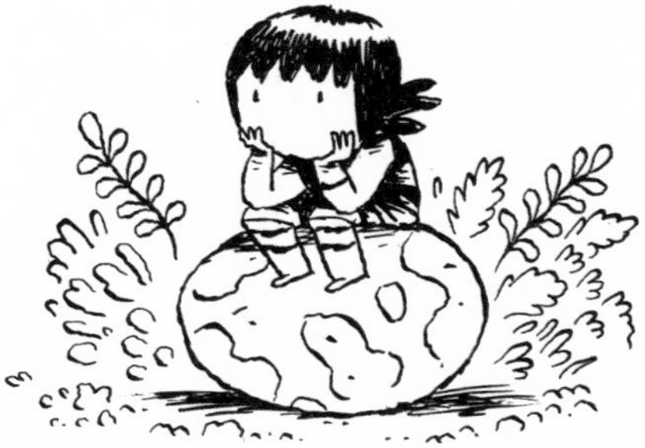

DRAWN AND QUARTERLY
D&Q

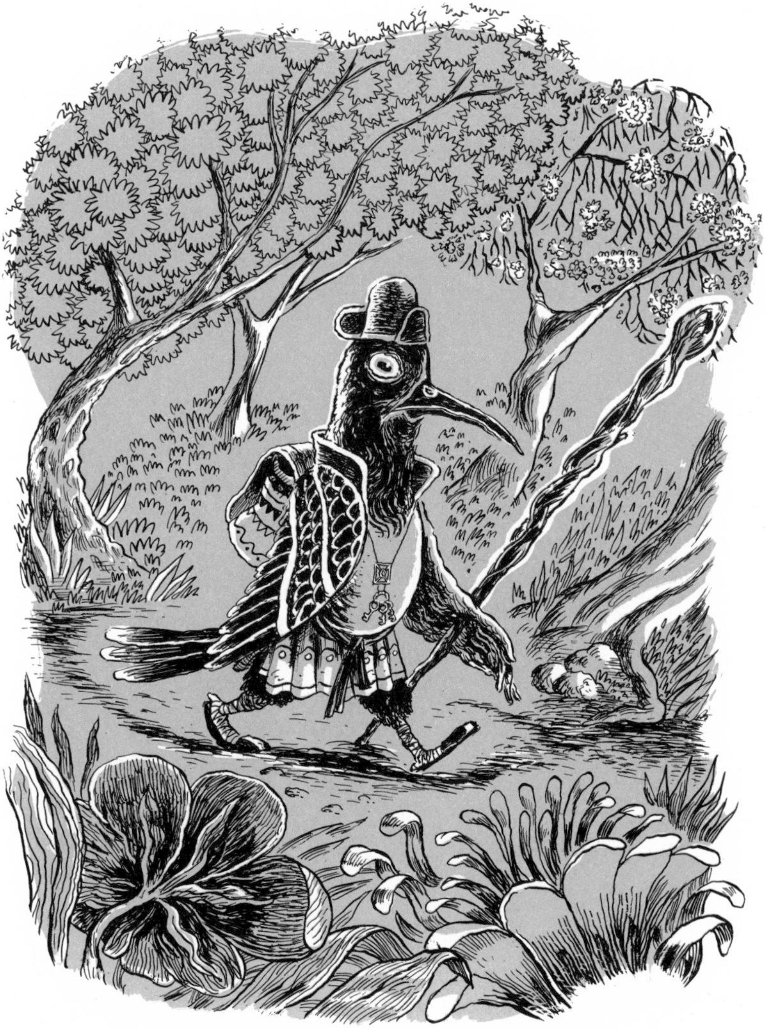

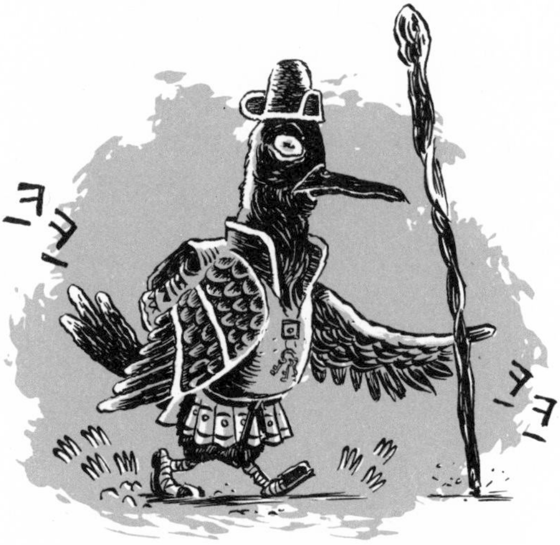
ㅋㅋ
ㅋㅋ

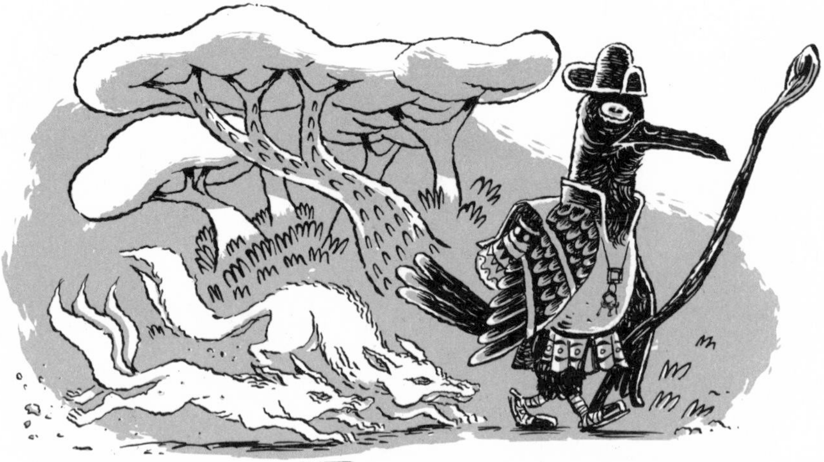

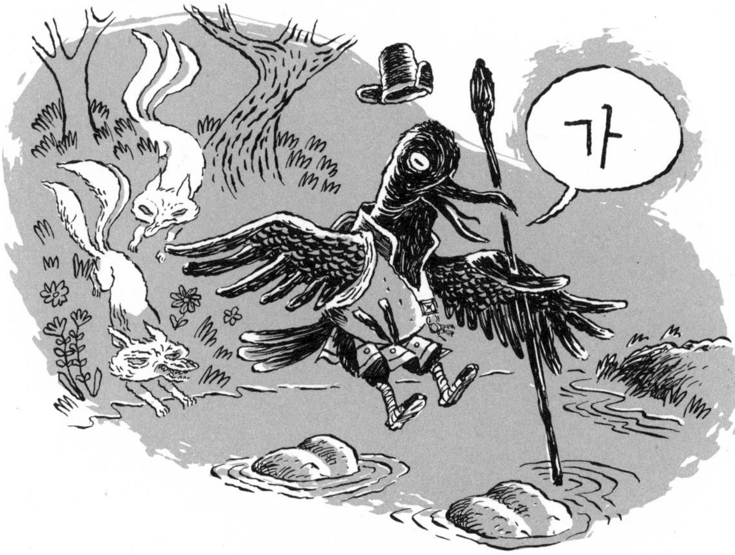
가

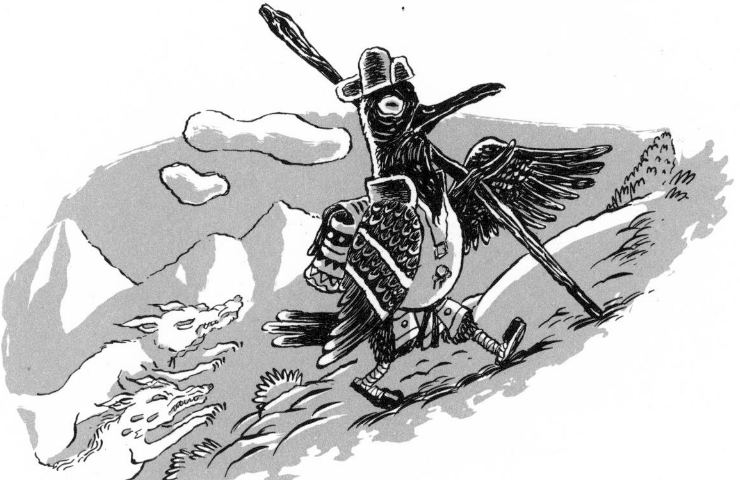

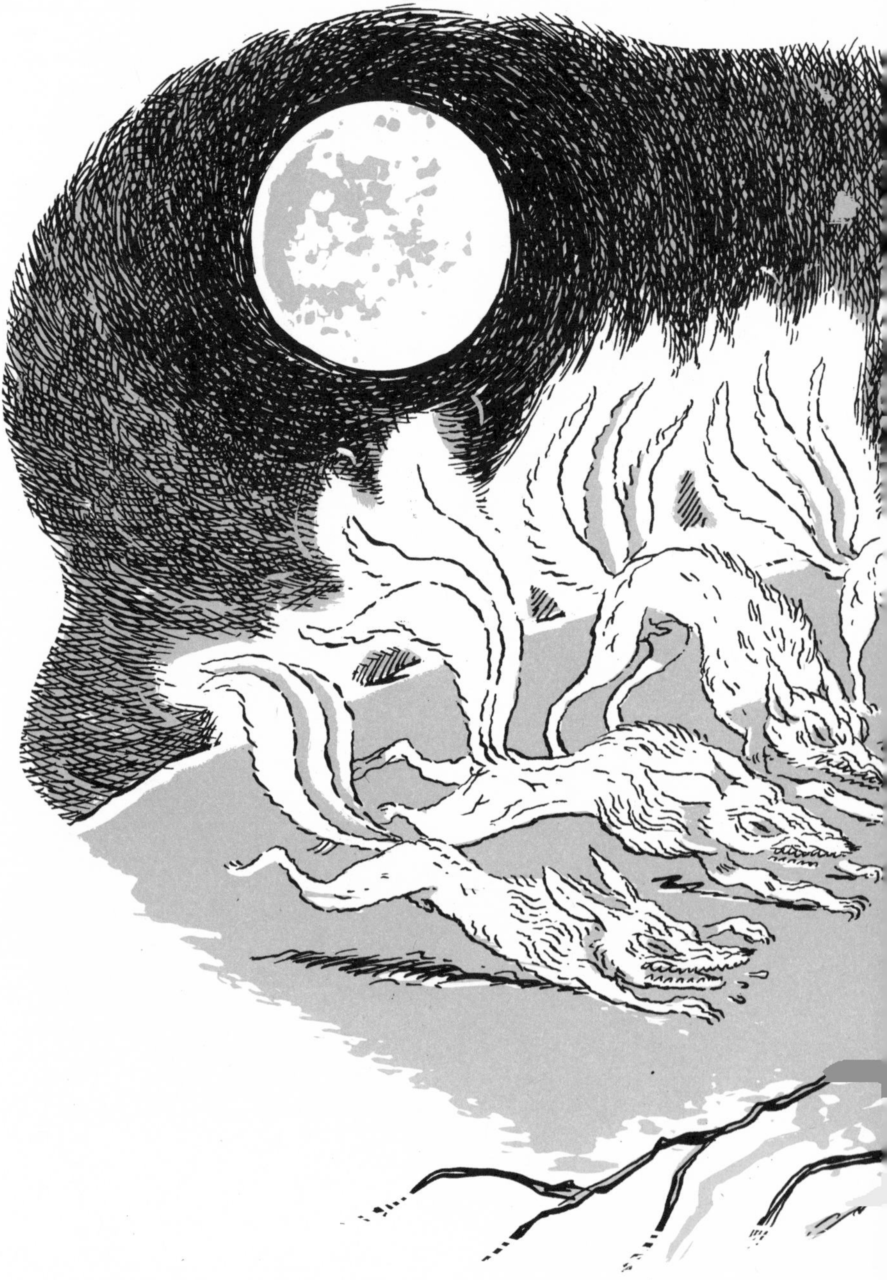

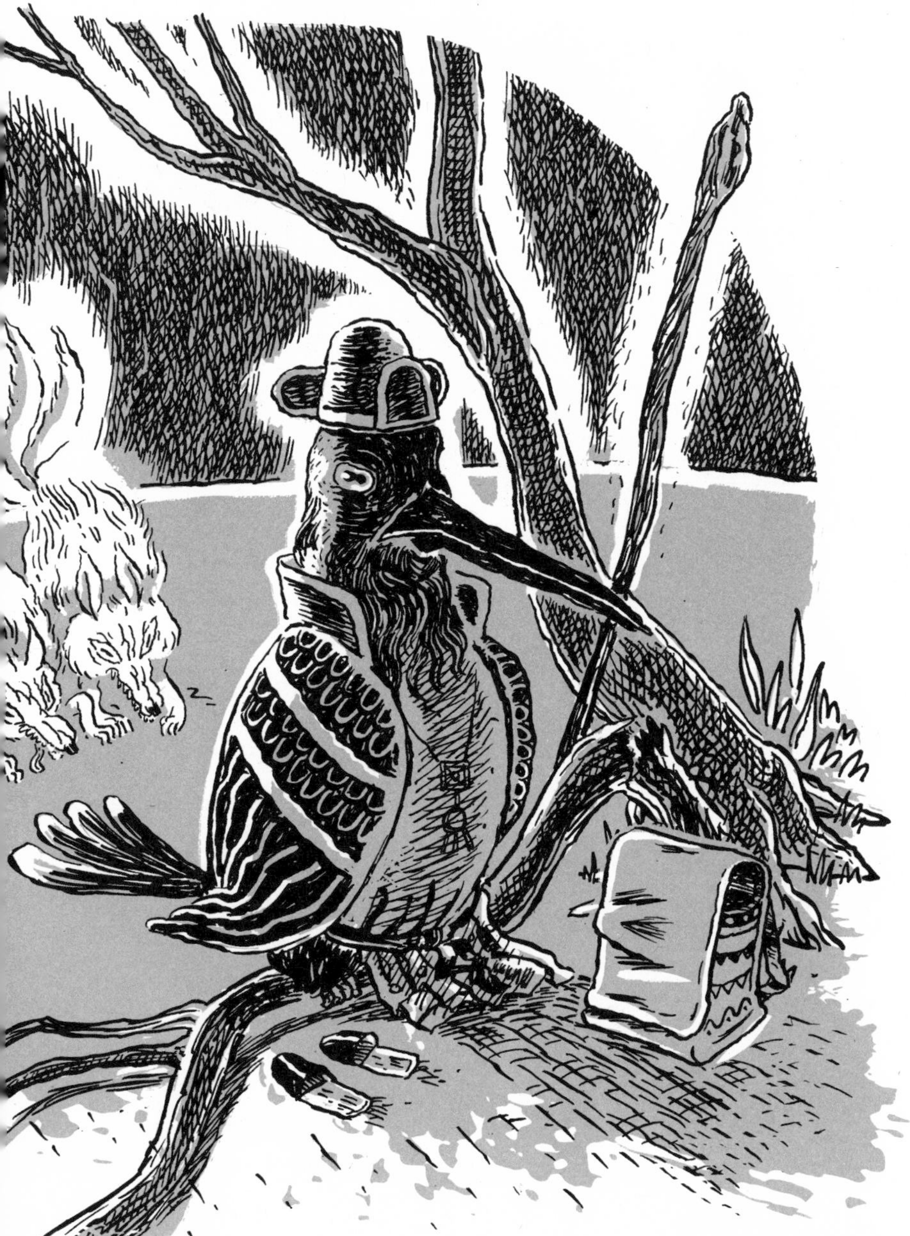

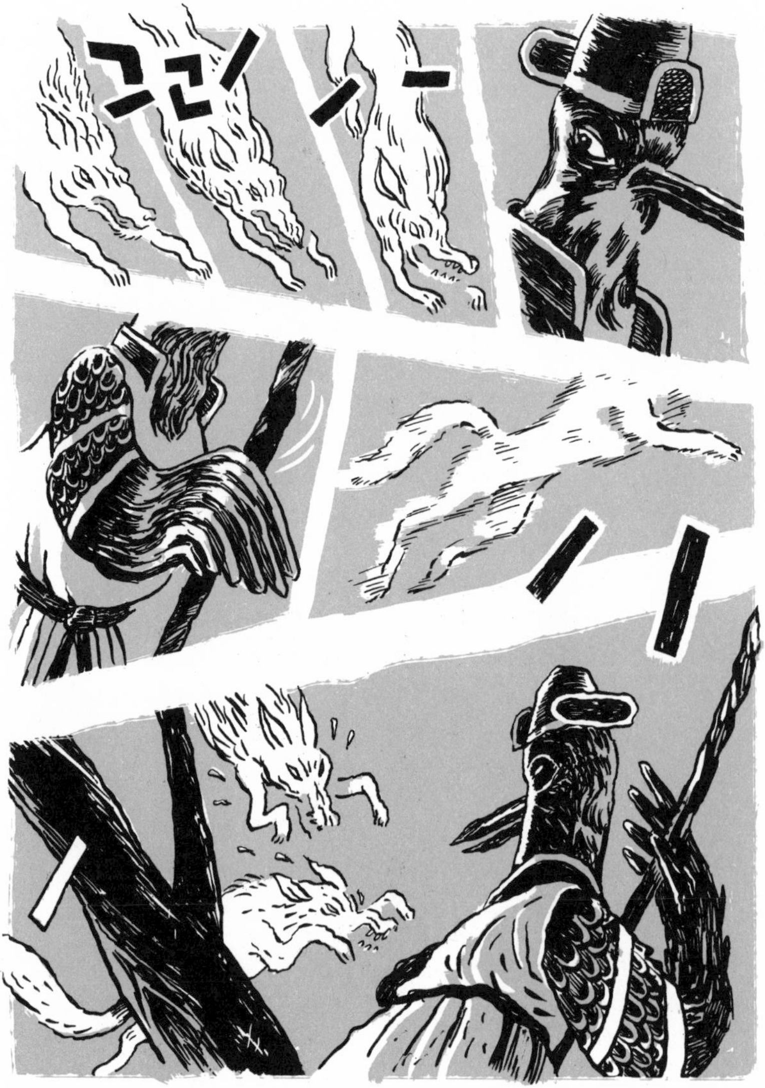

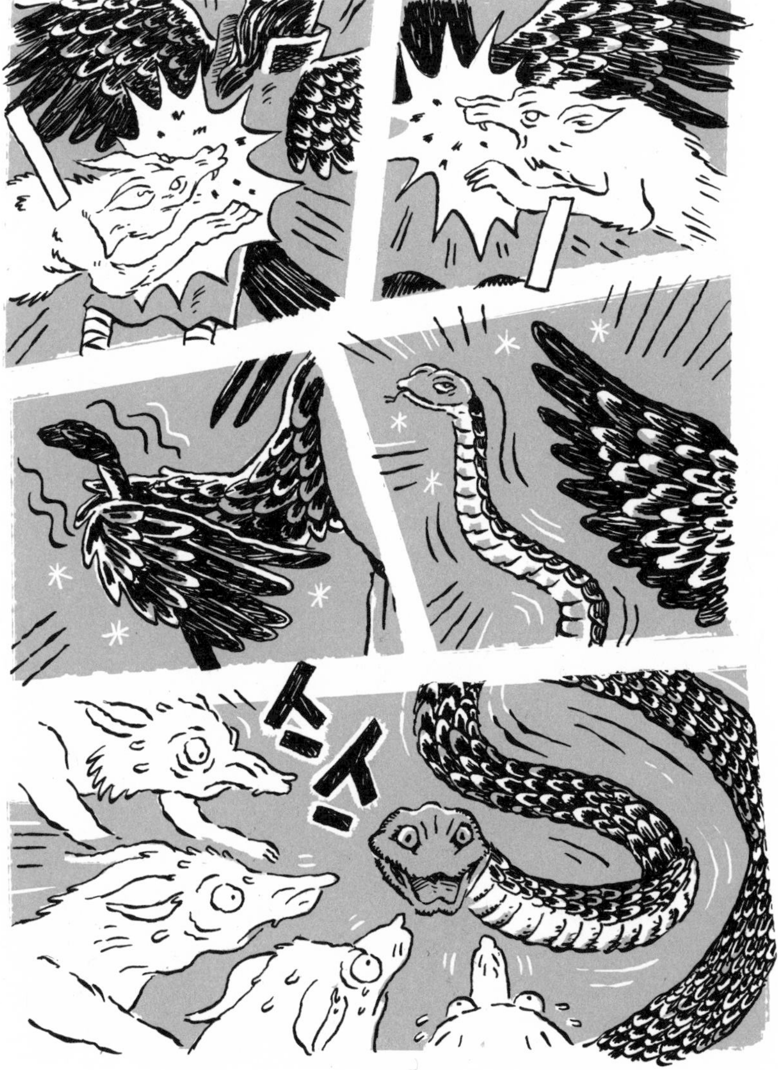

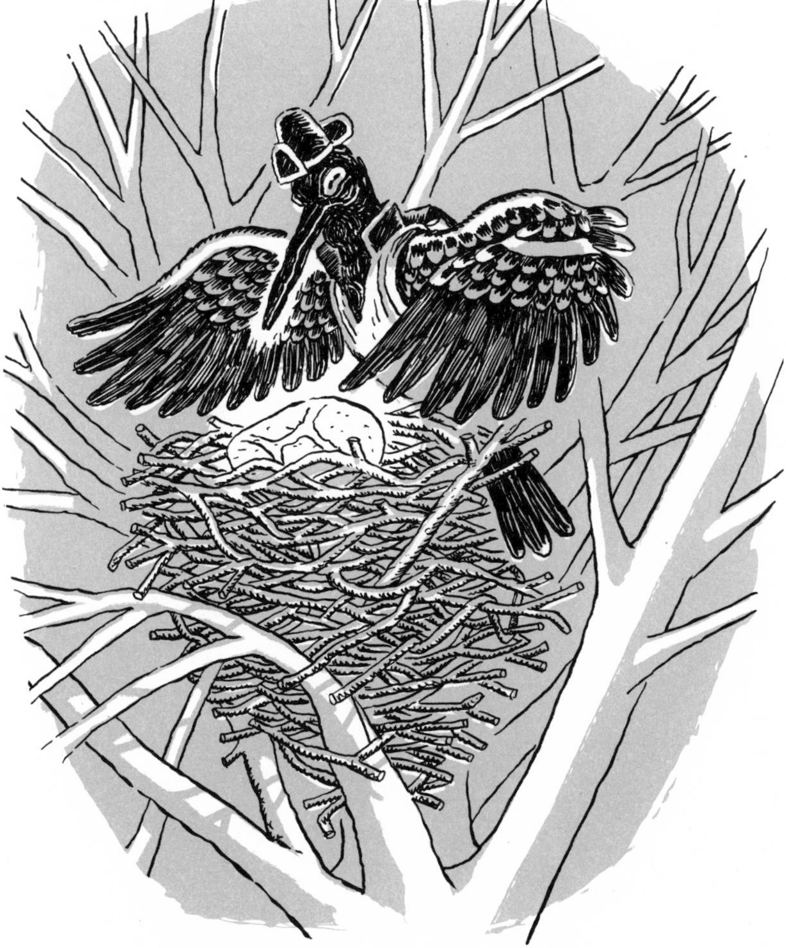

I.

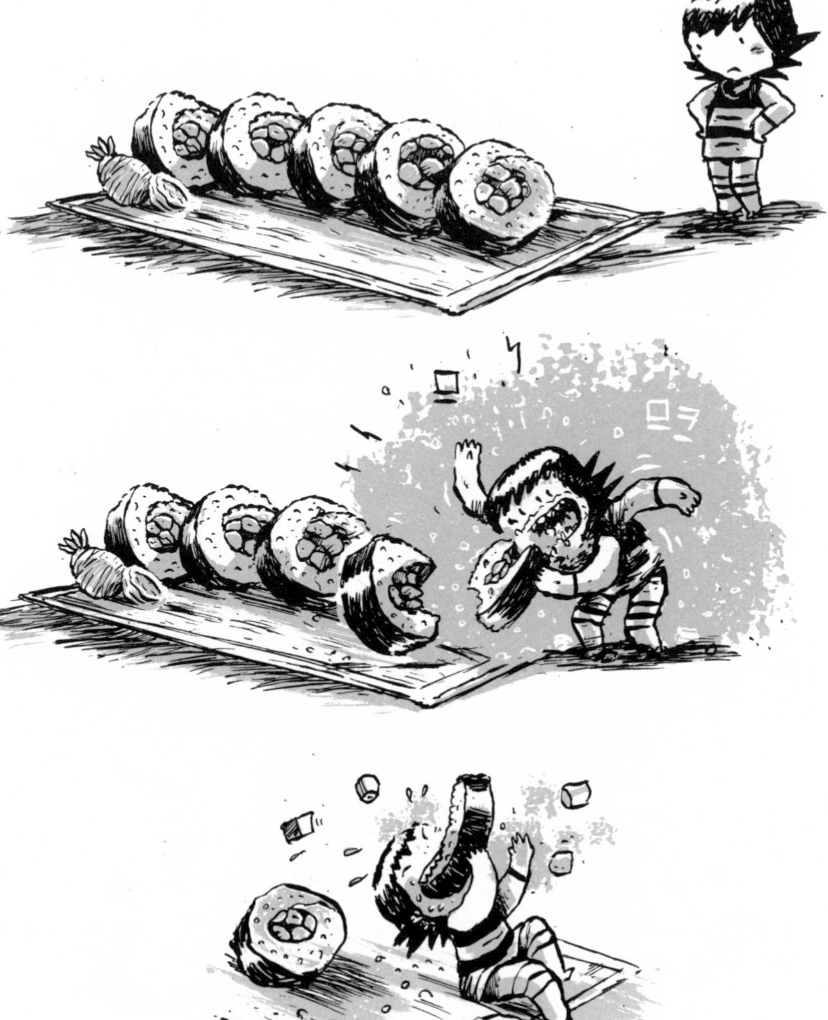

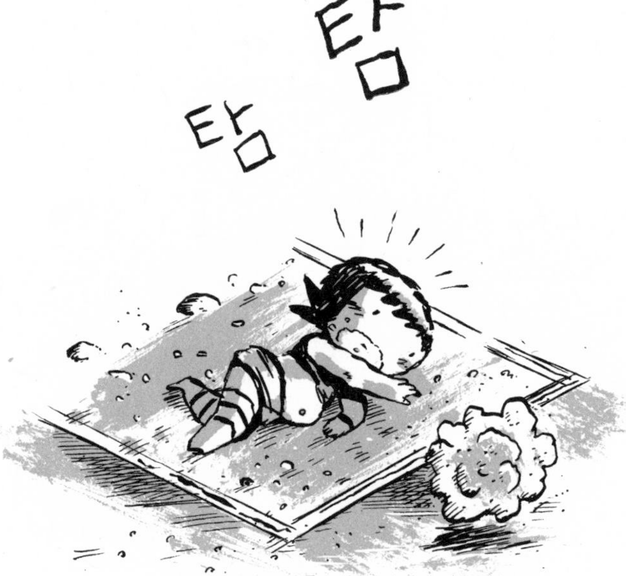

탐
탐

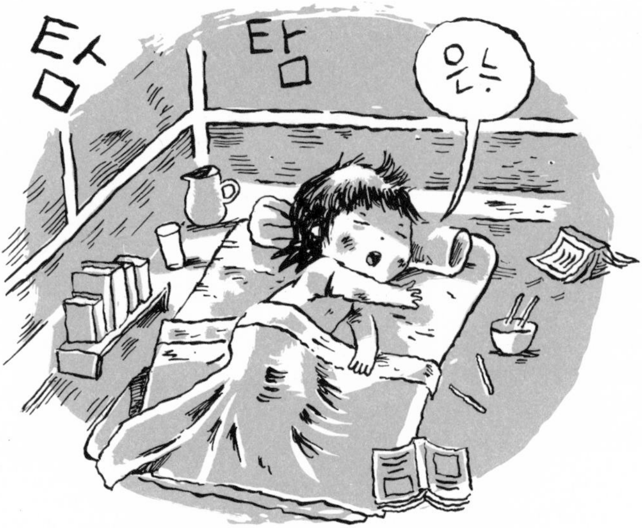
탐
탐
은느.

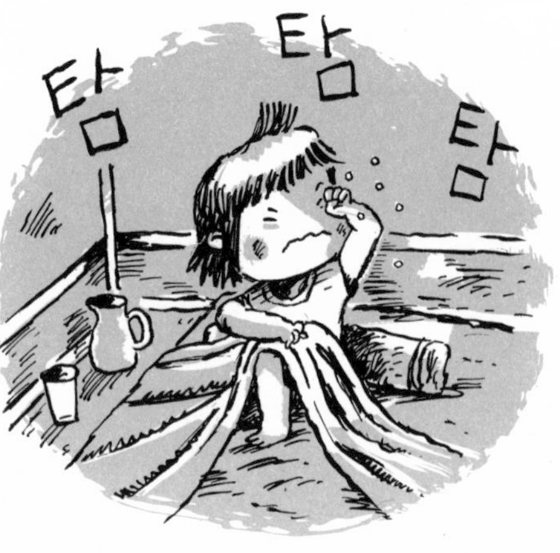
탐
탐
탐

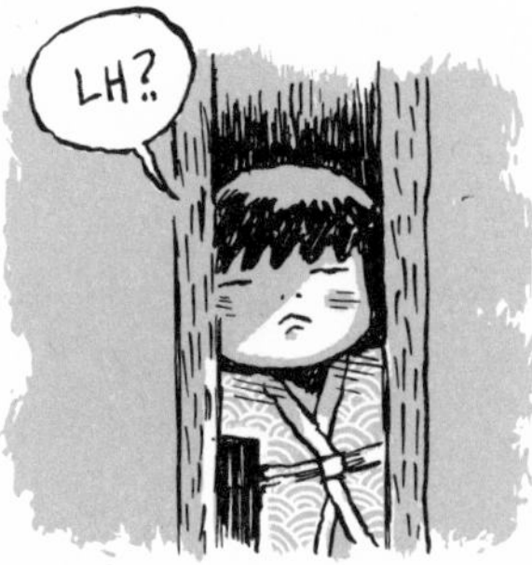
LH?

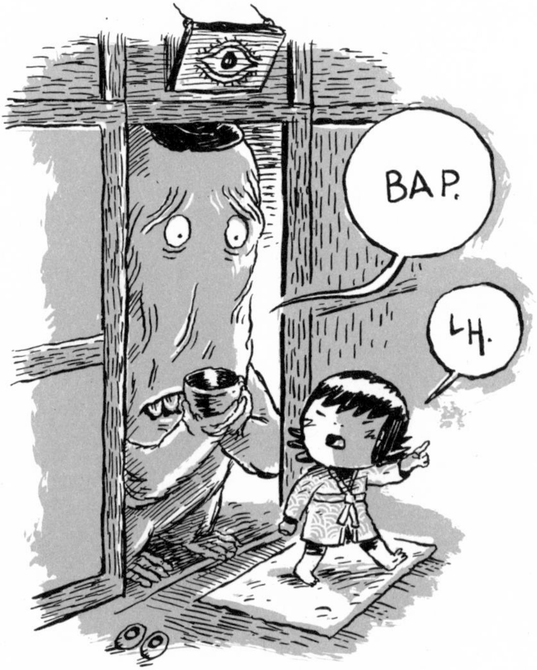
BAP.
LH.

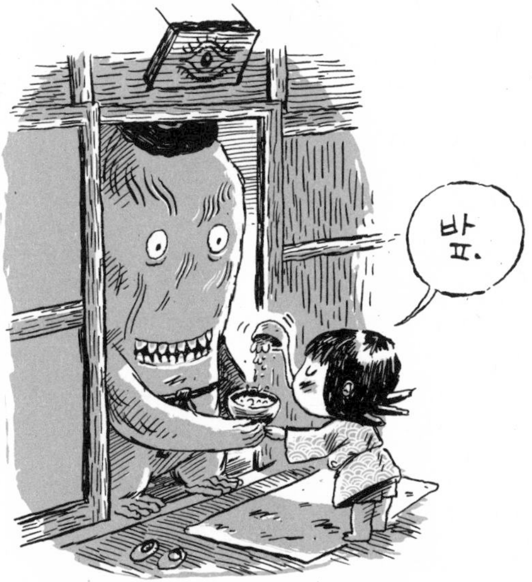
밮.

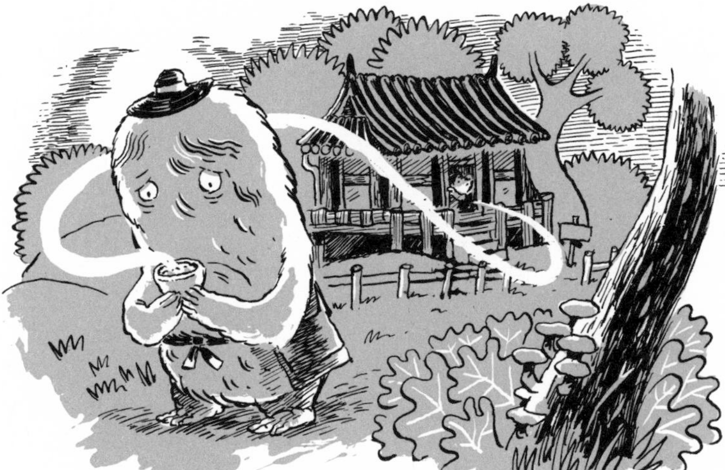

shlp.

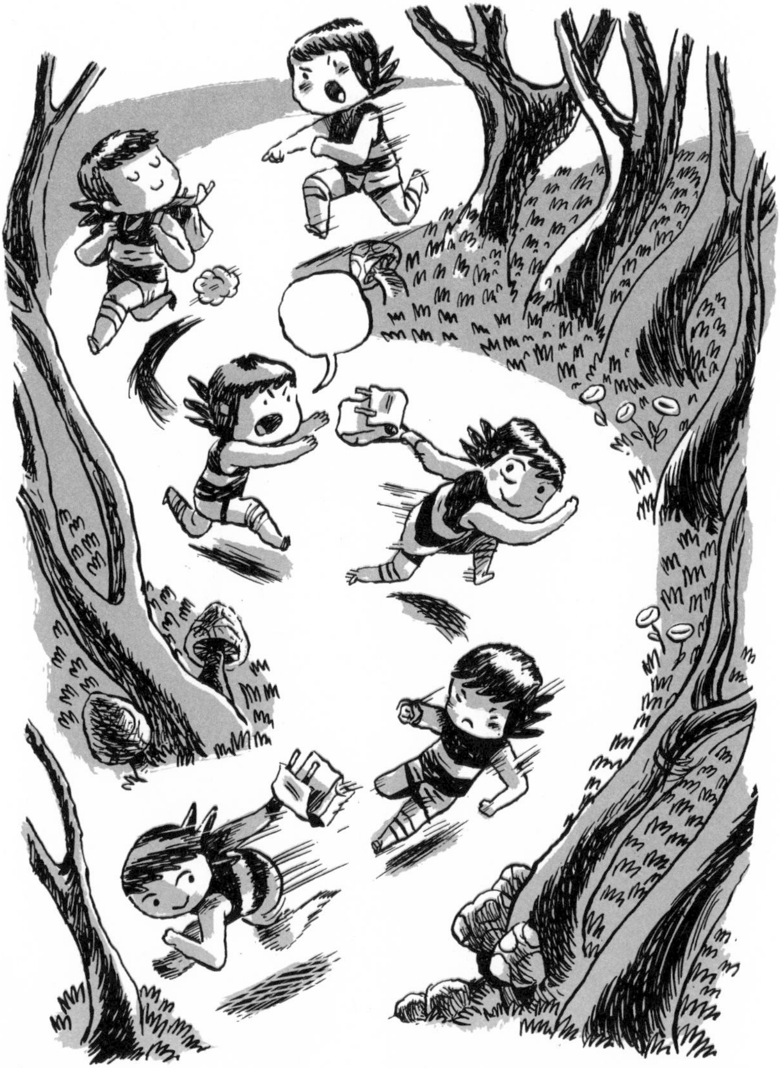

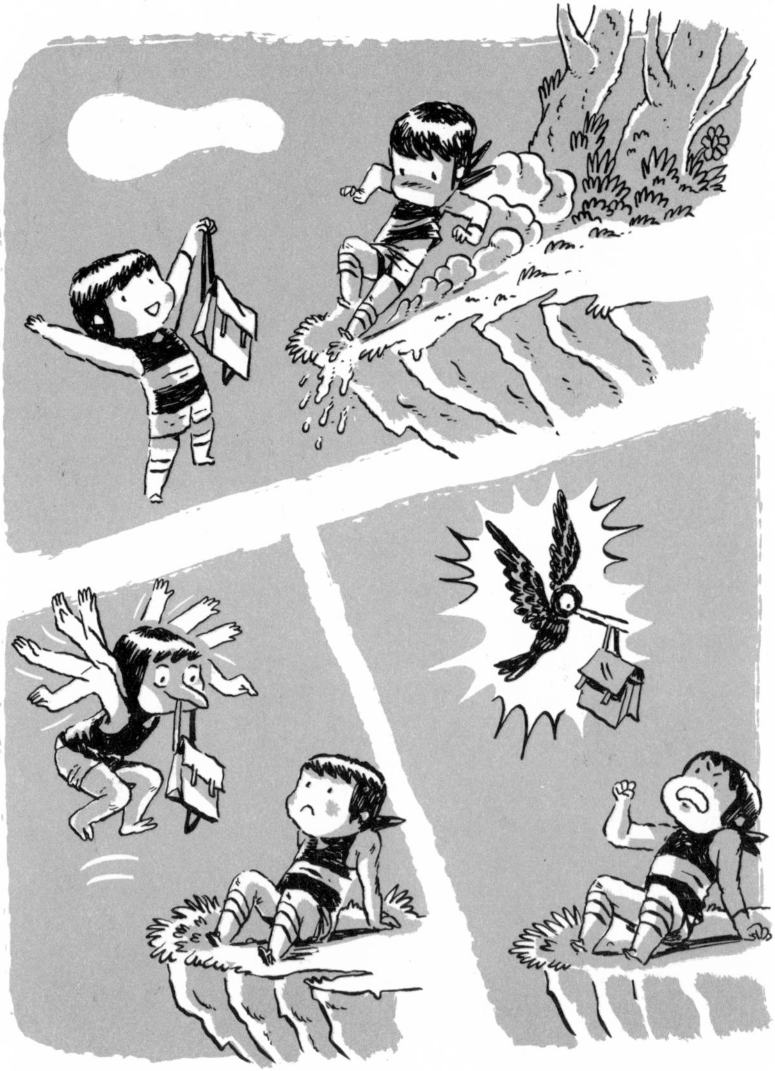

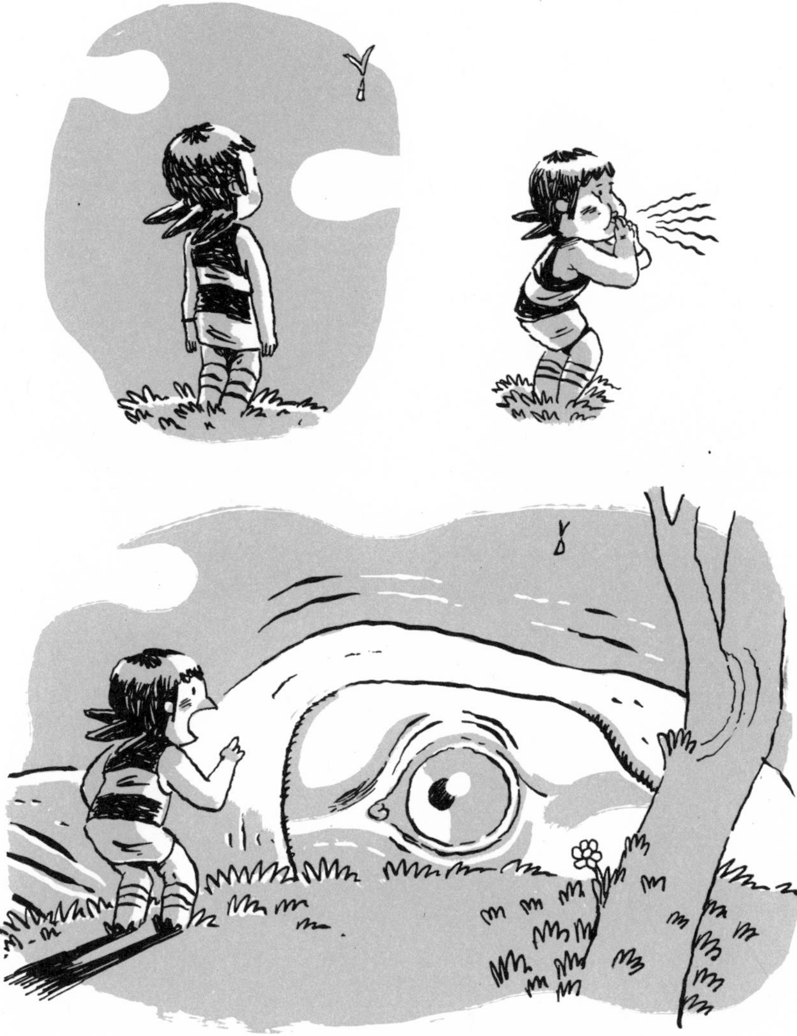

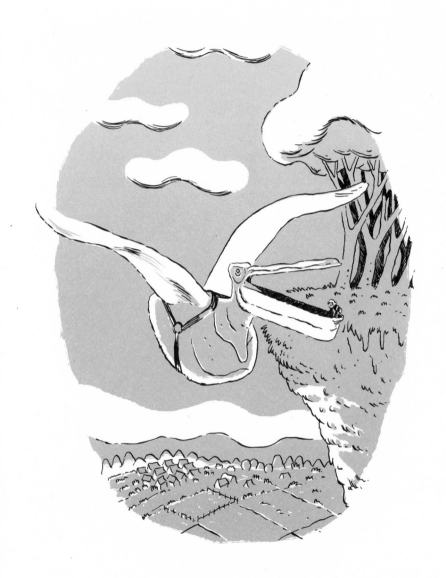

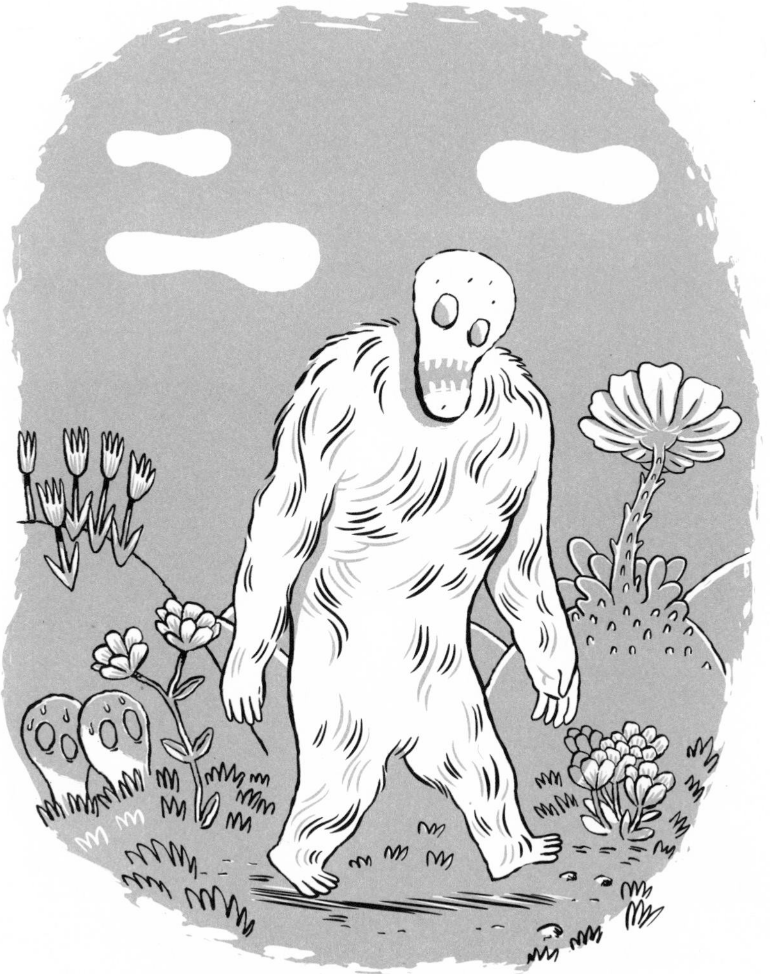

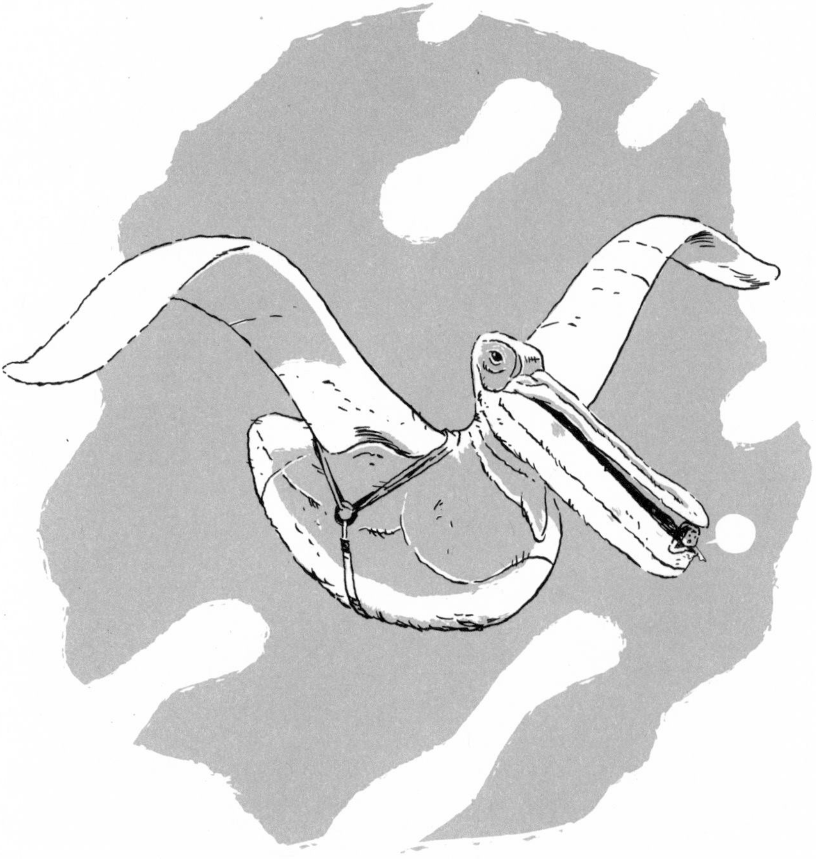

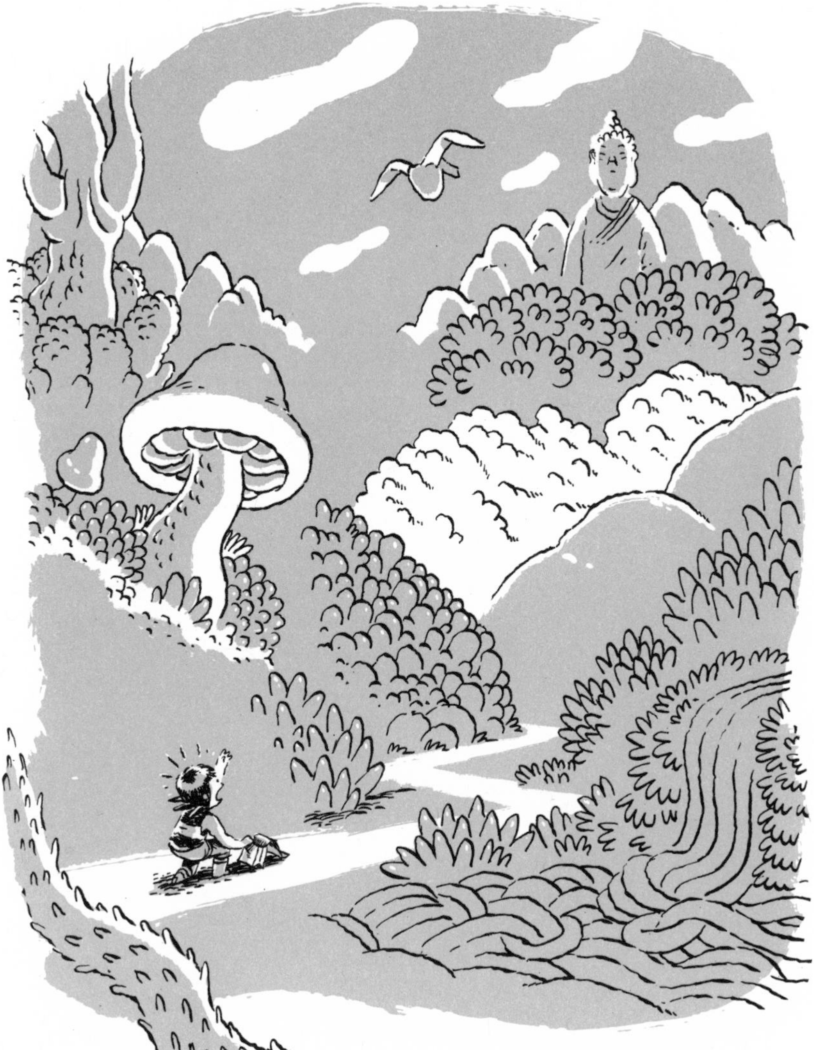

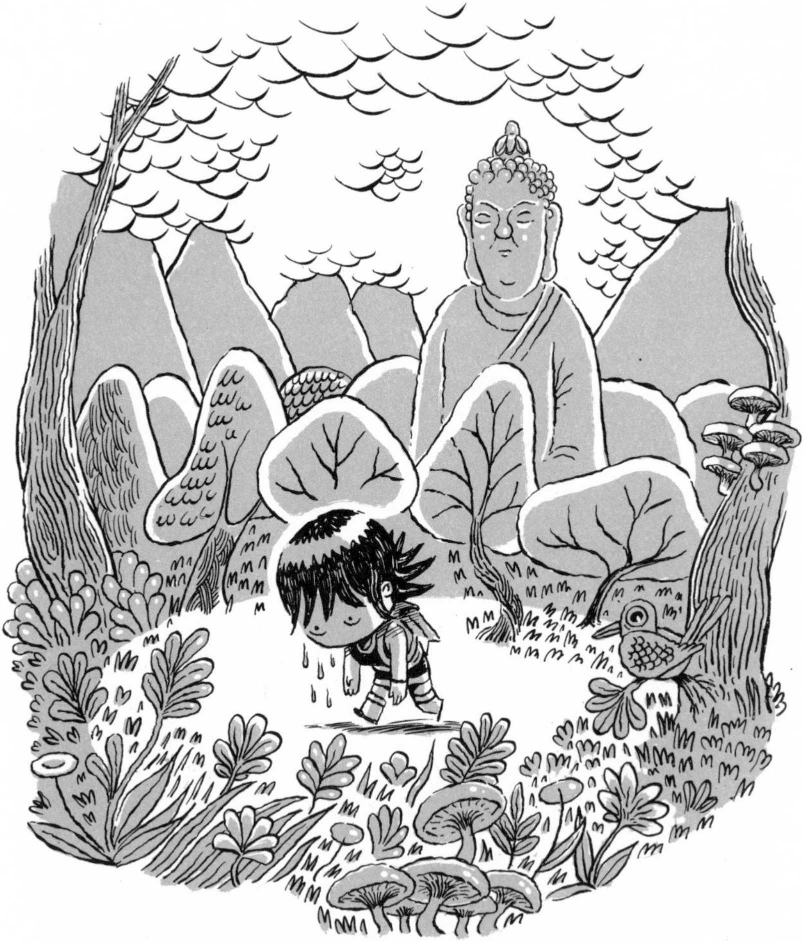

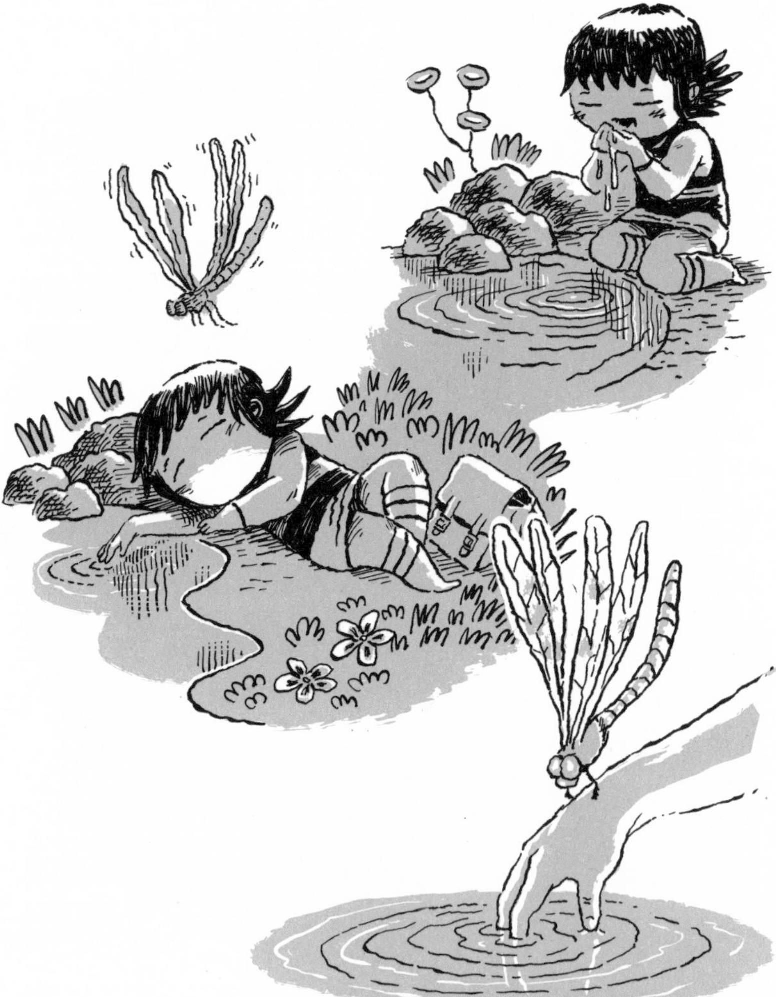

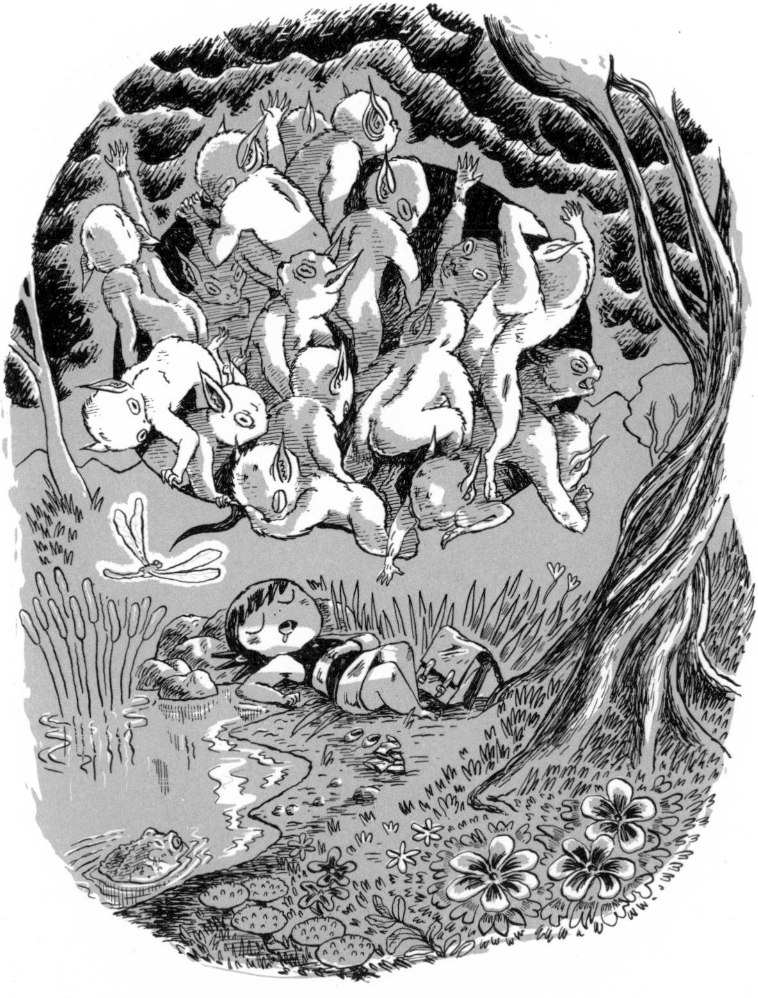

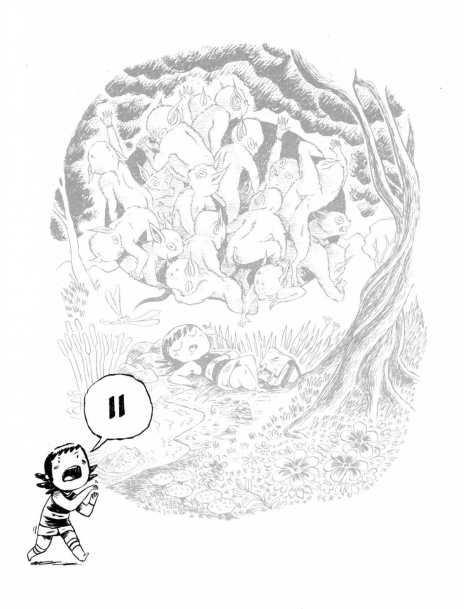

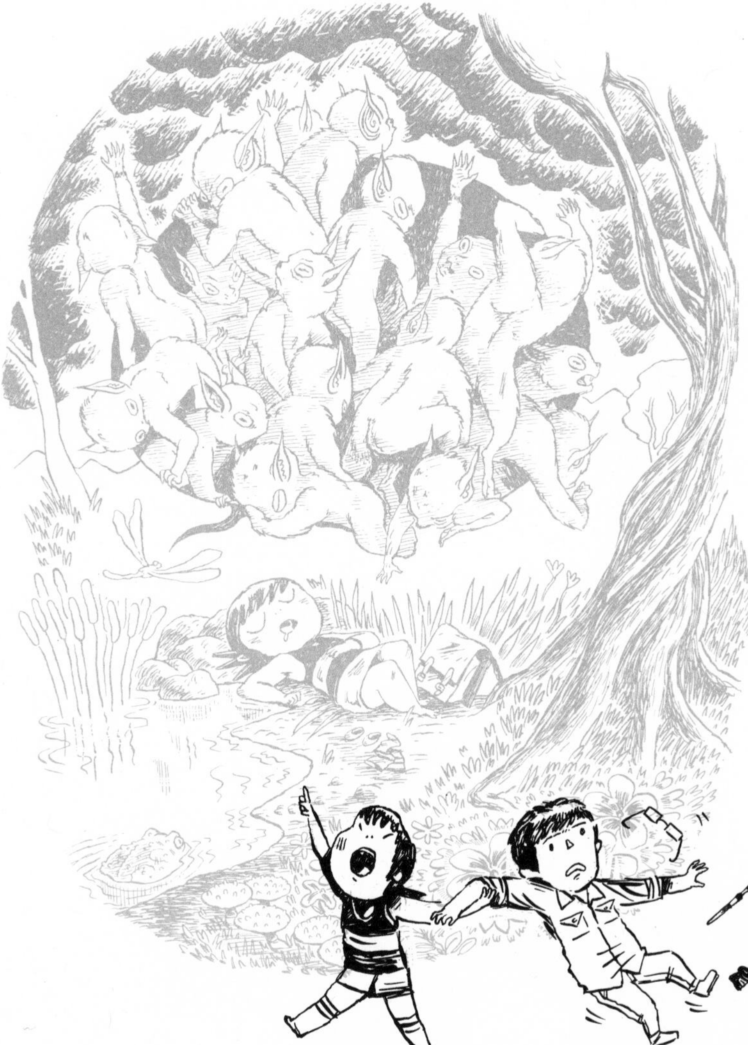

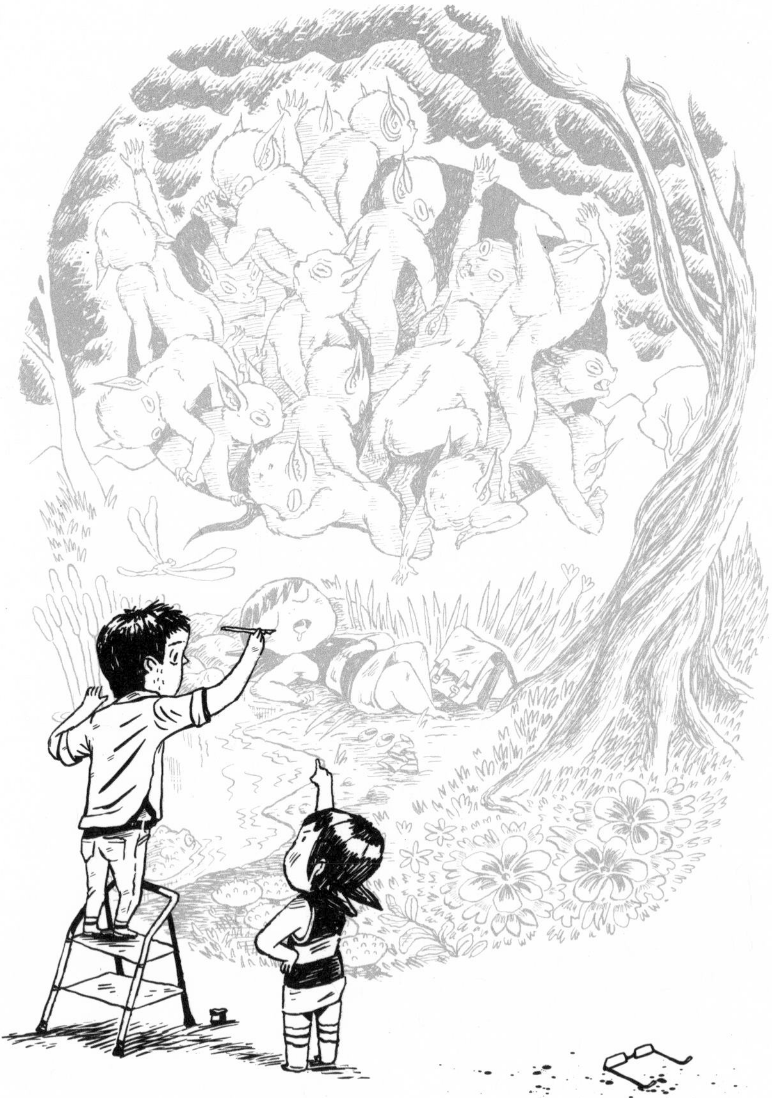

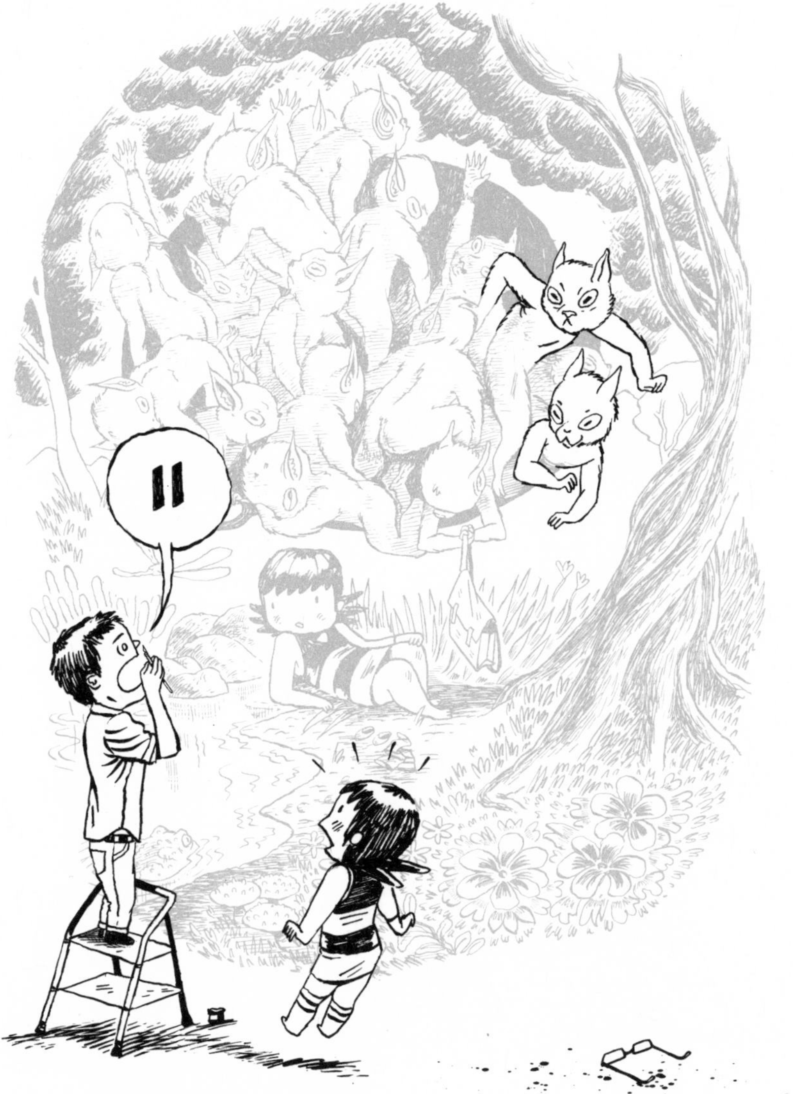

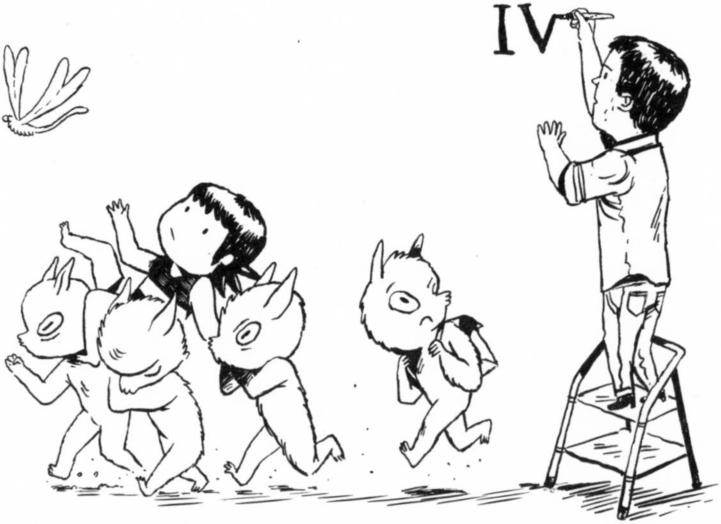
IV

IV.

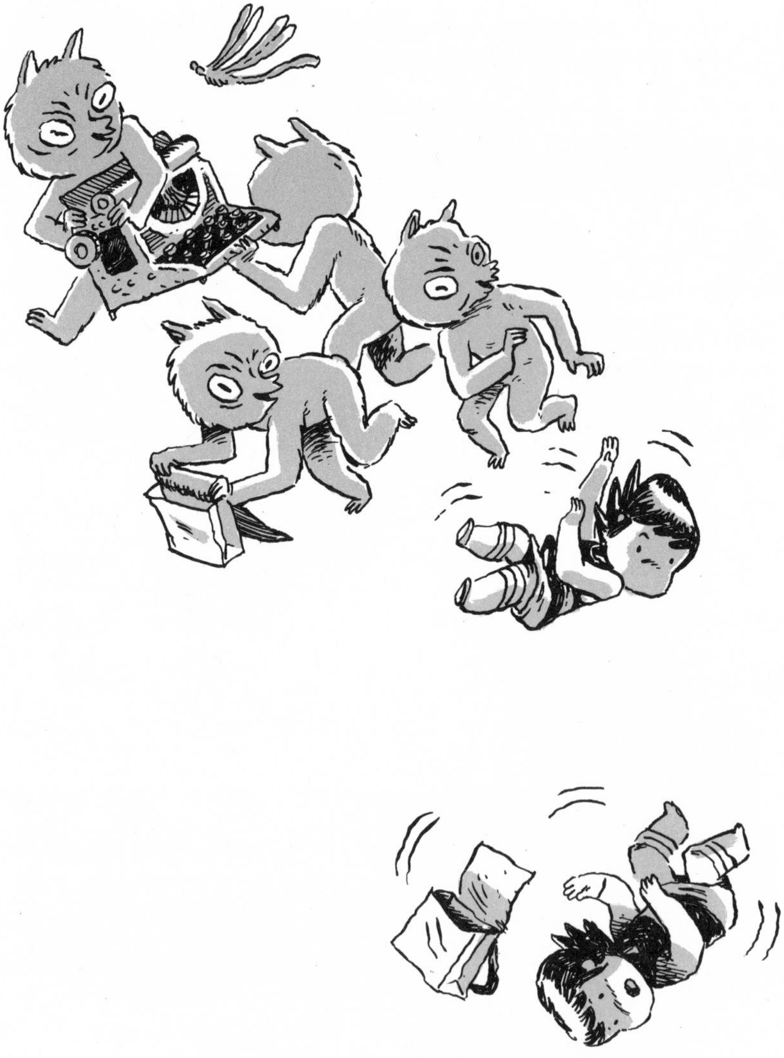

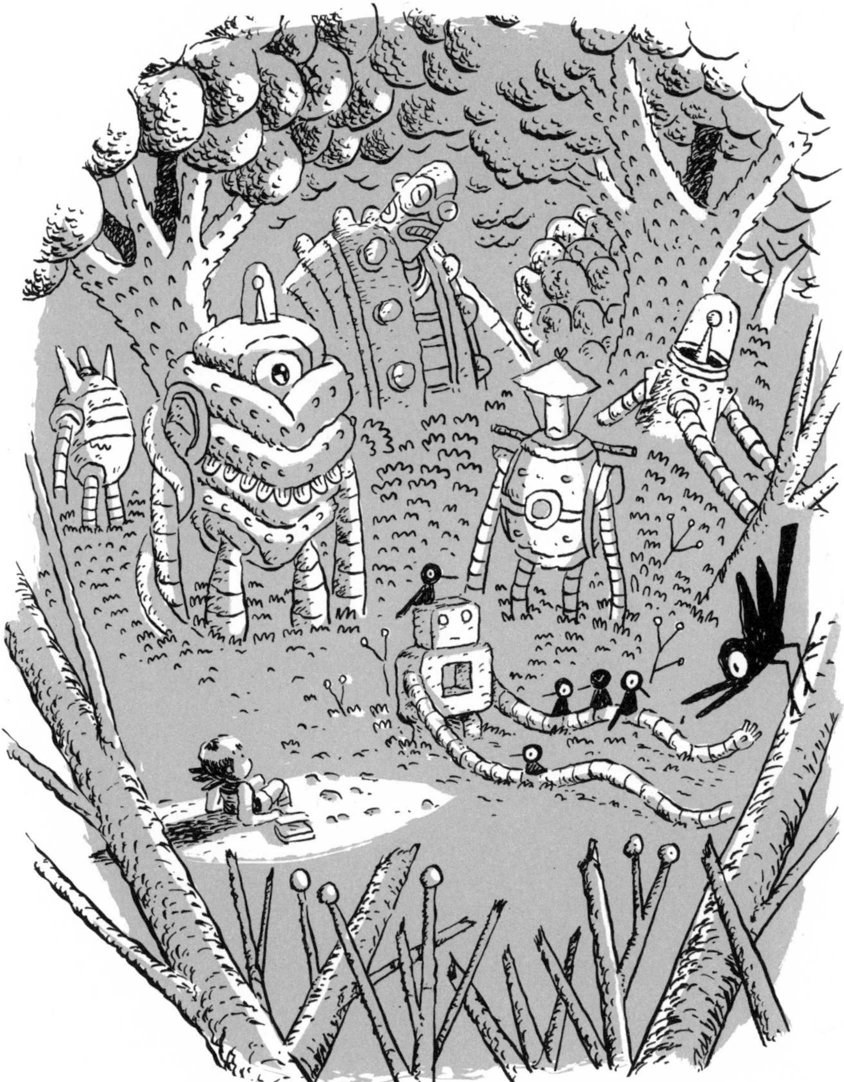

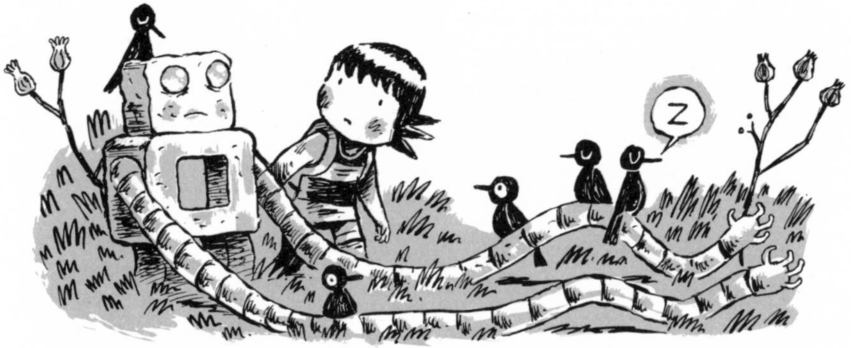
Z

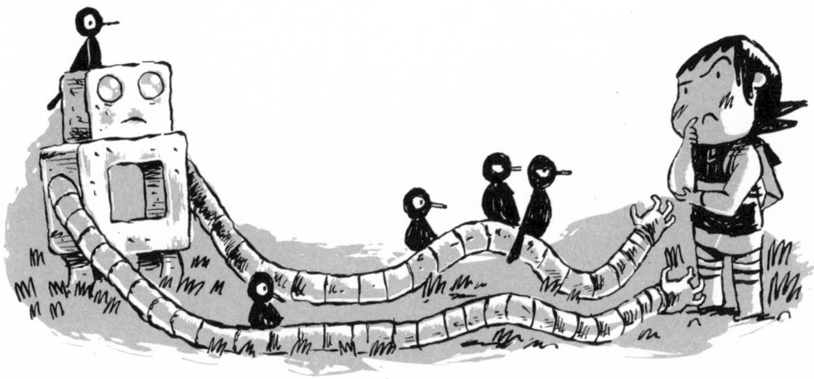

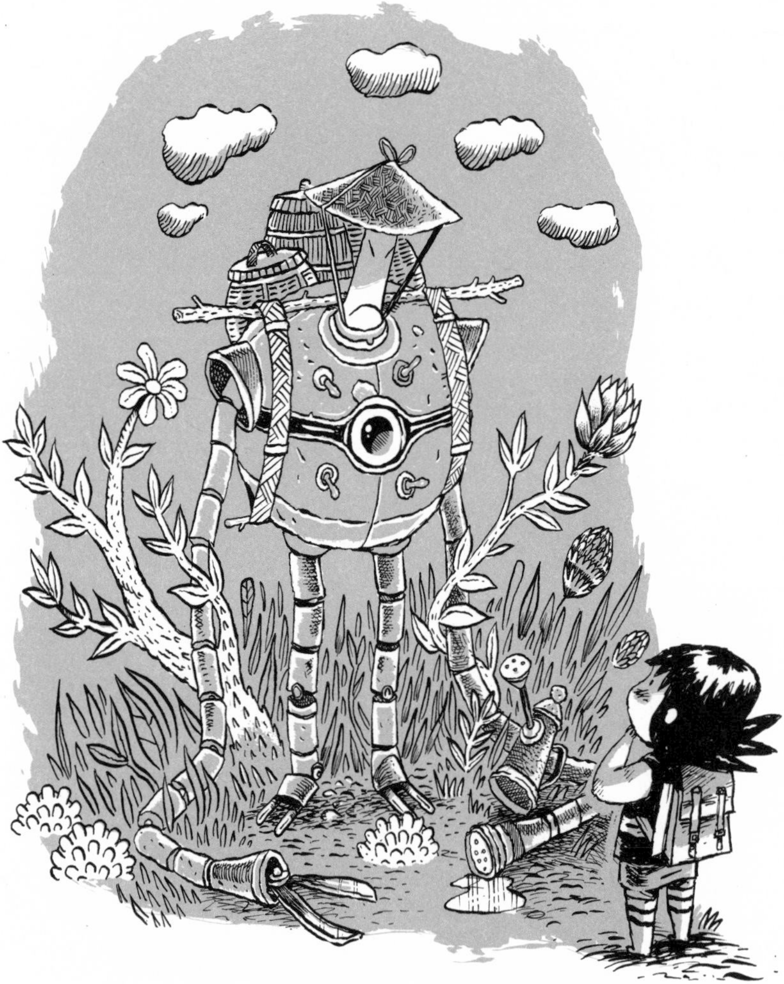

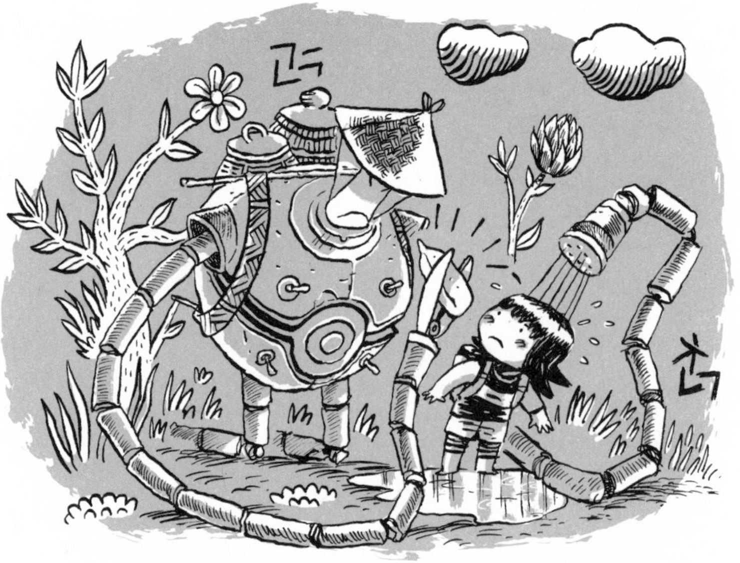

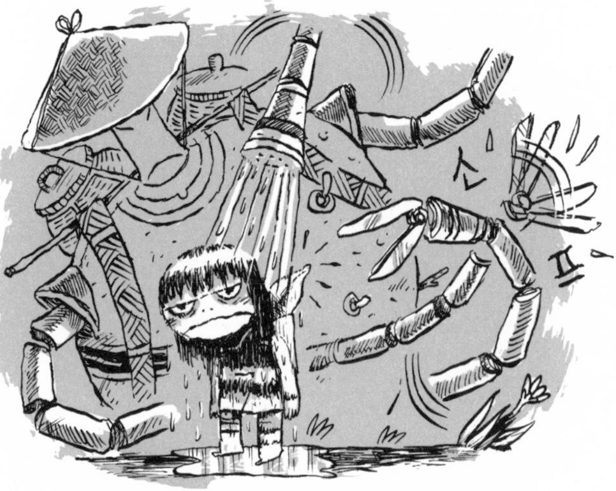

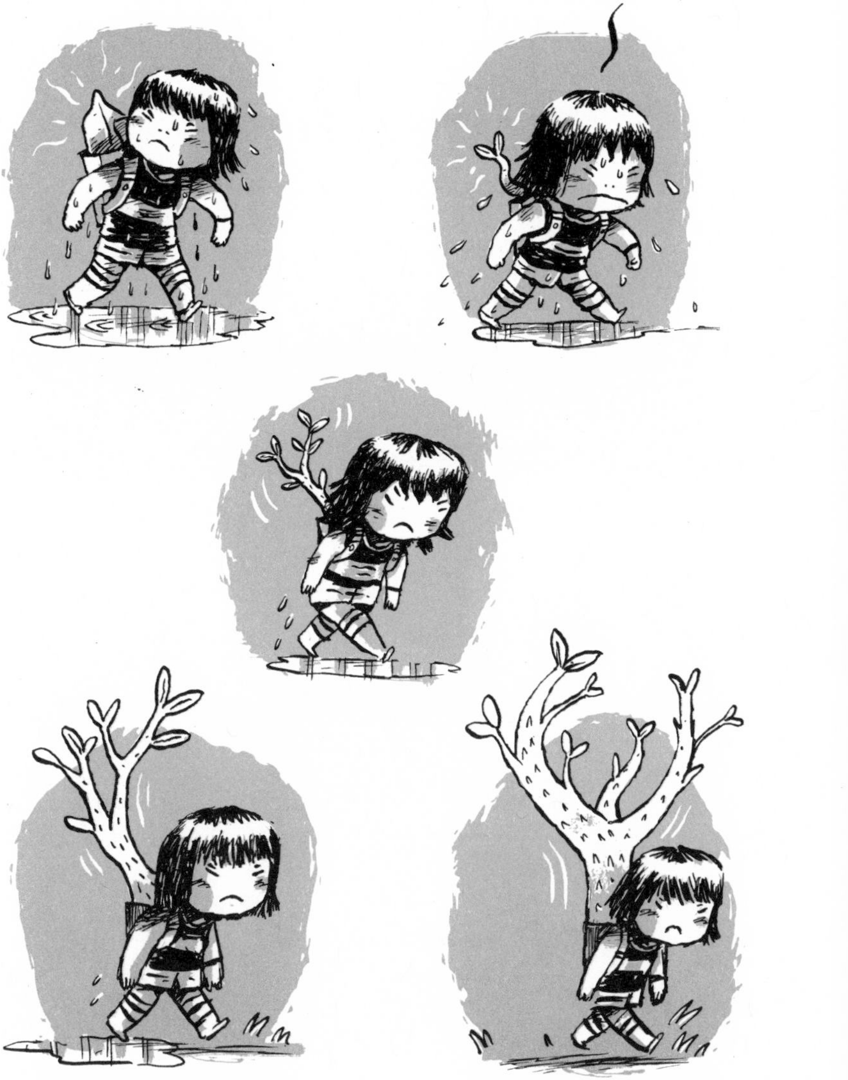

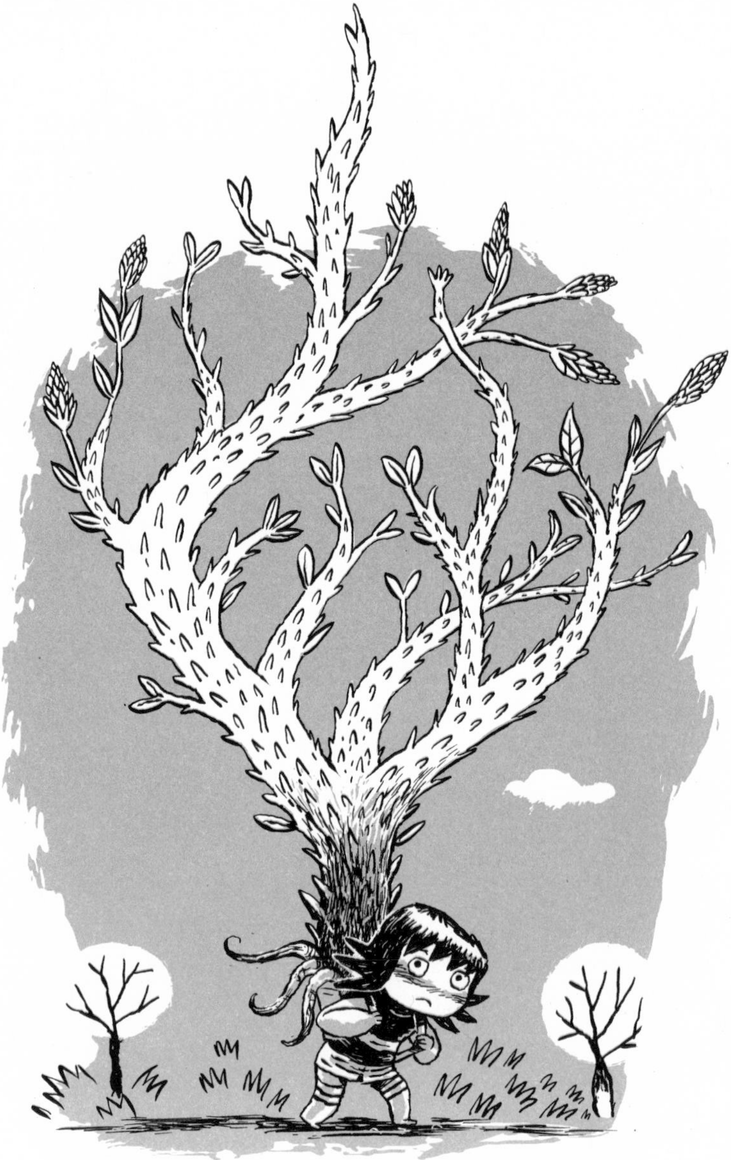

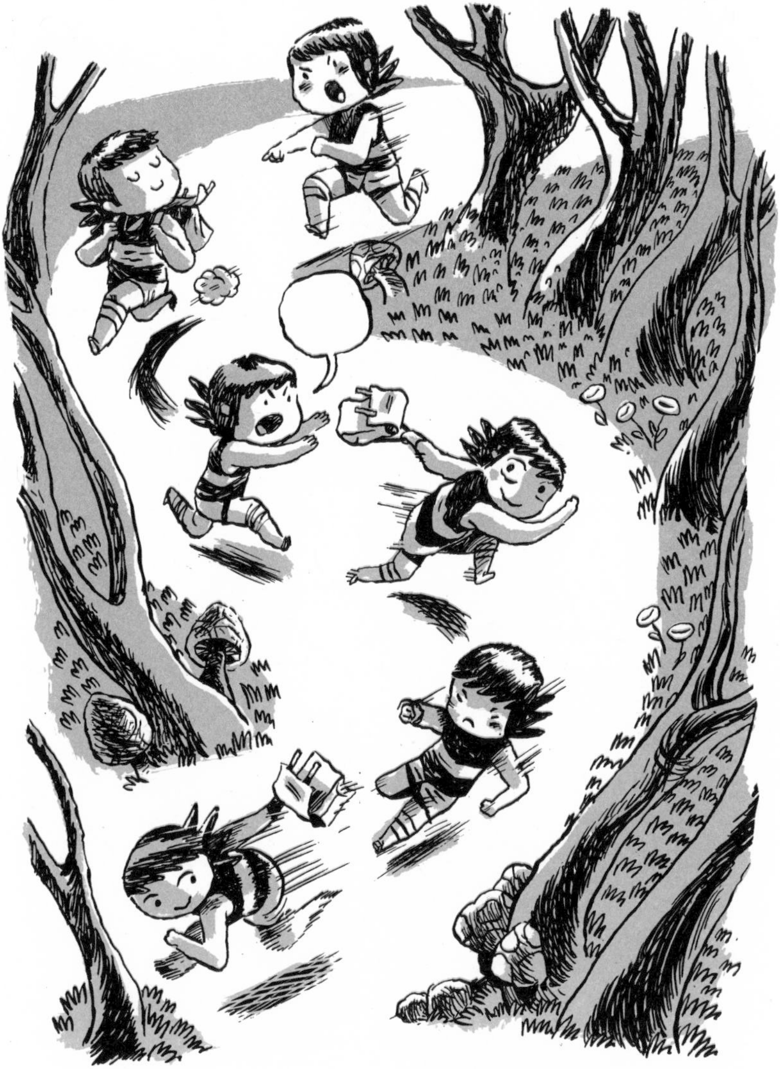

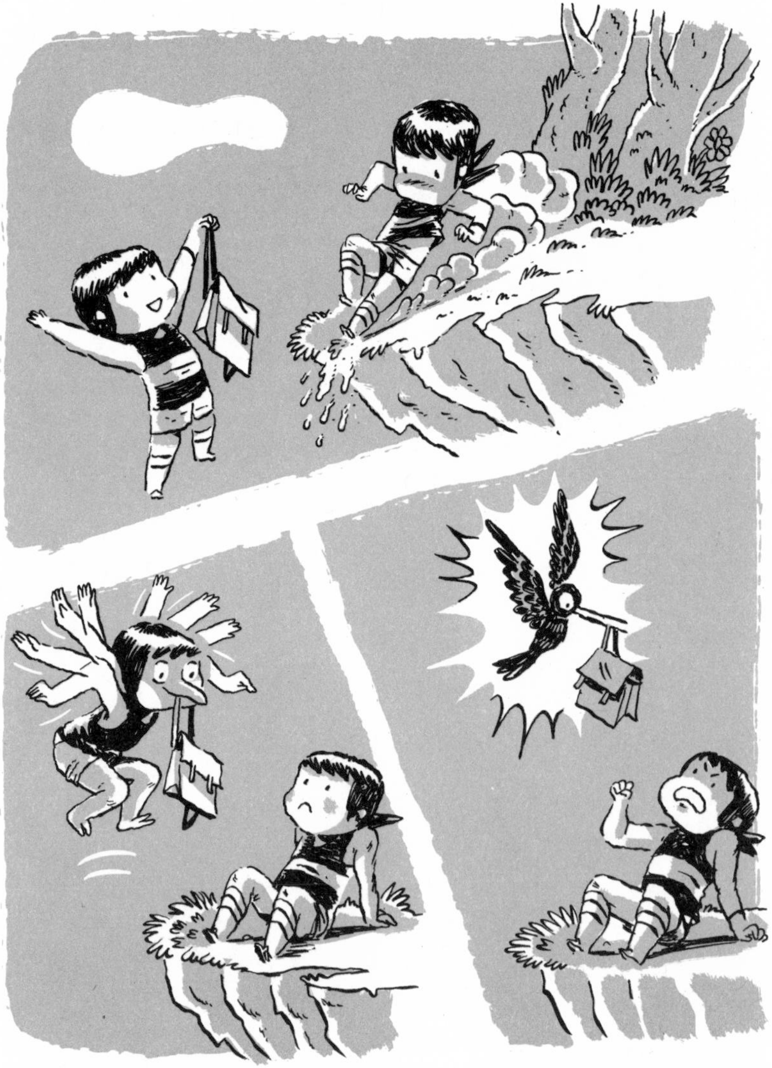

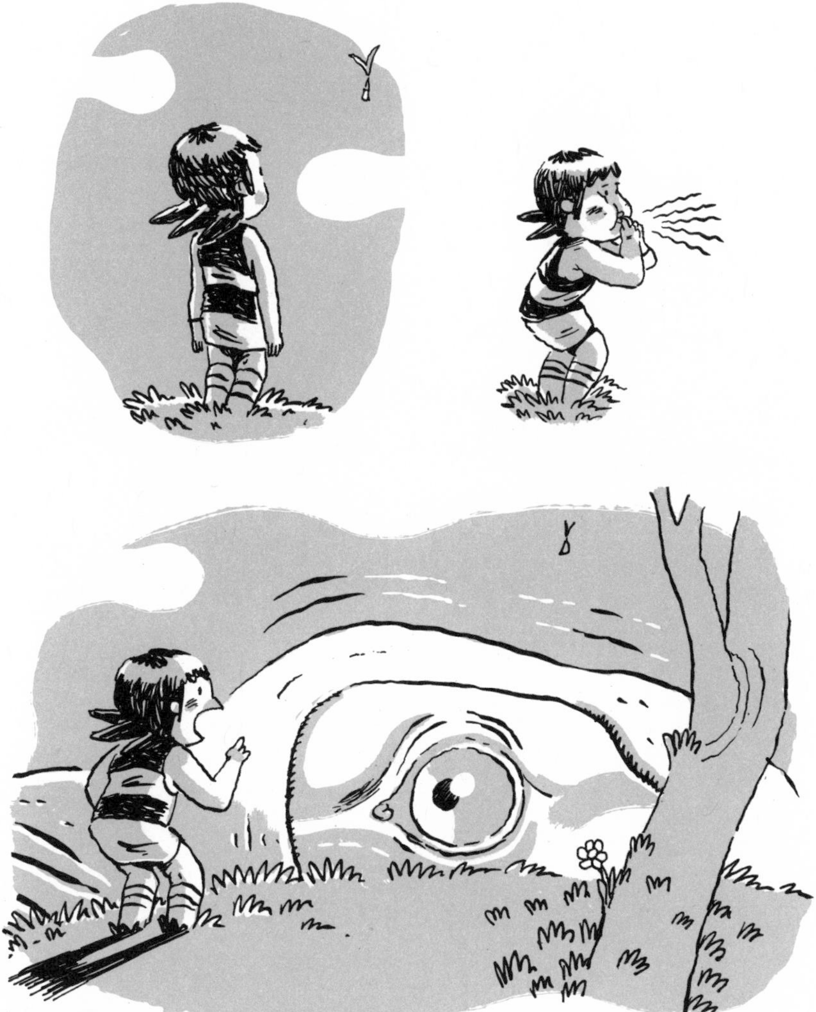

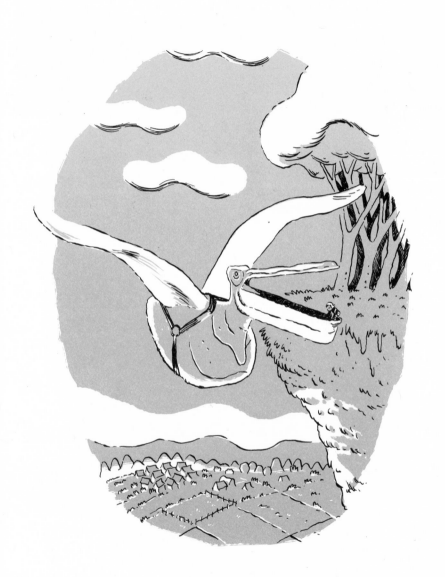

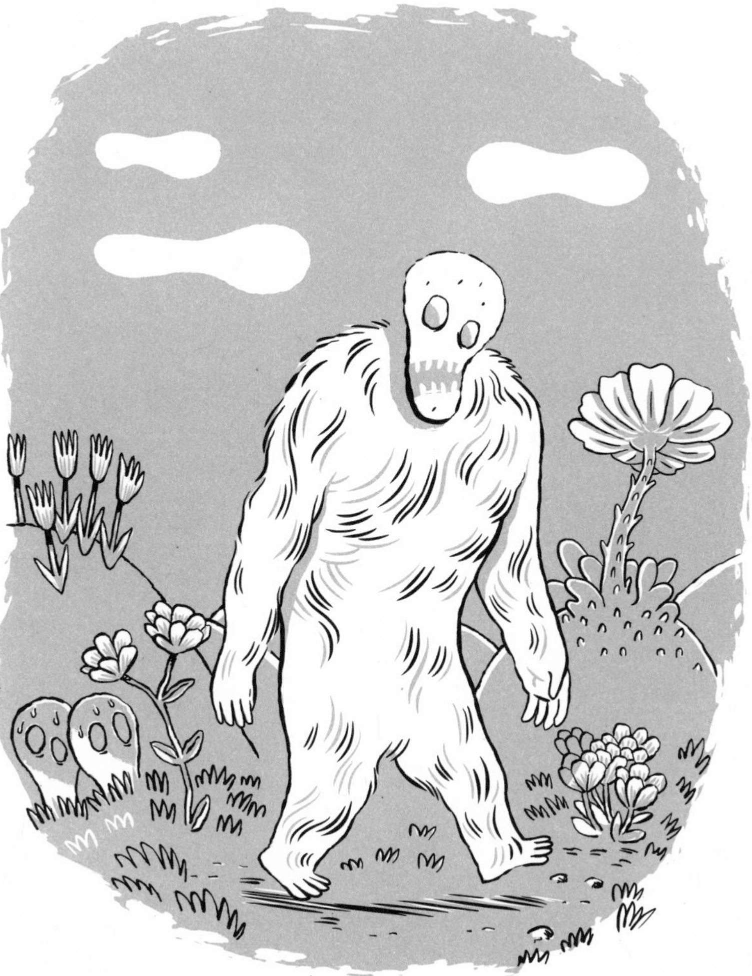

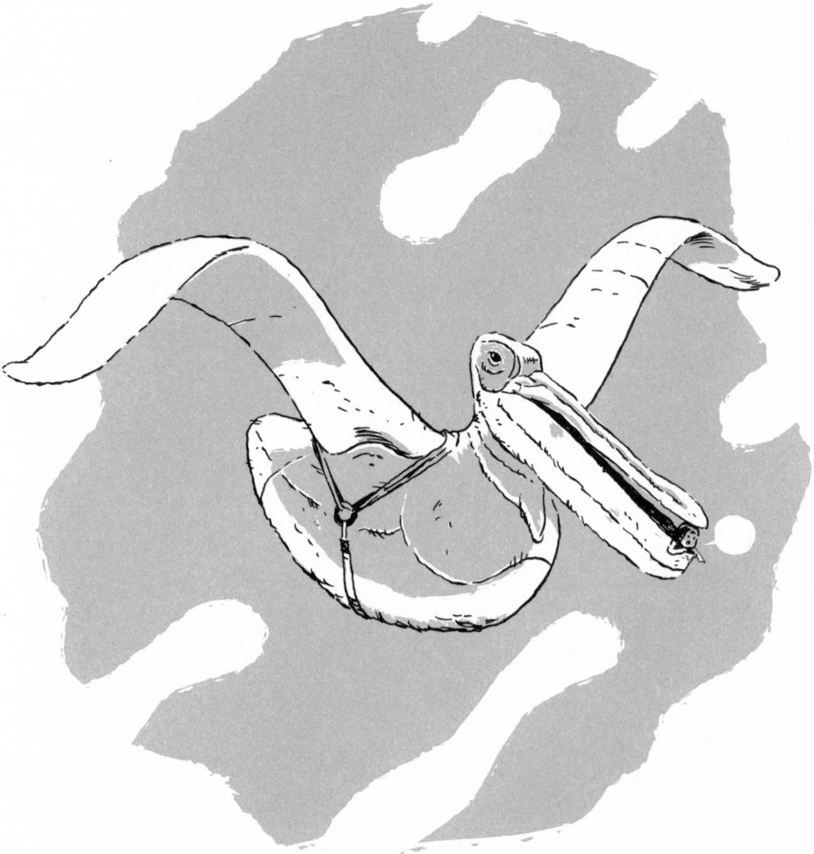

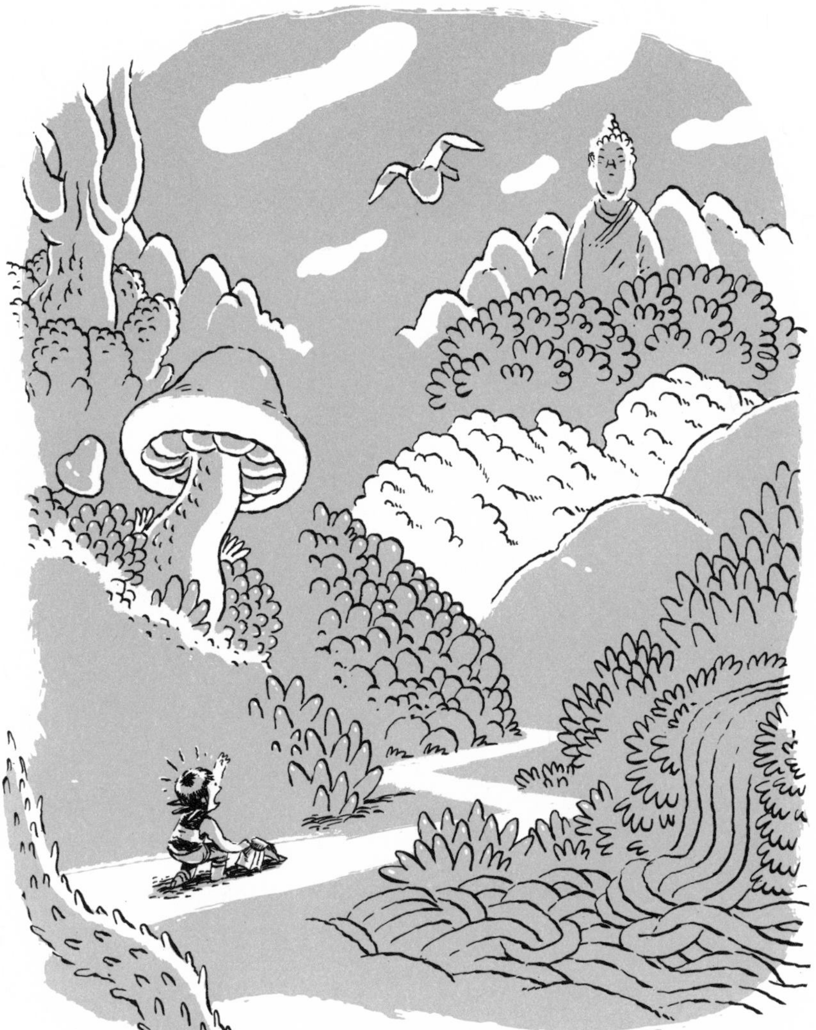

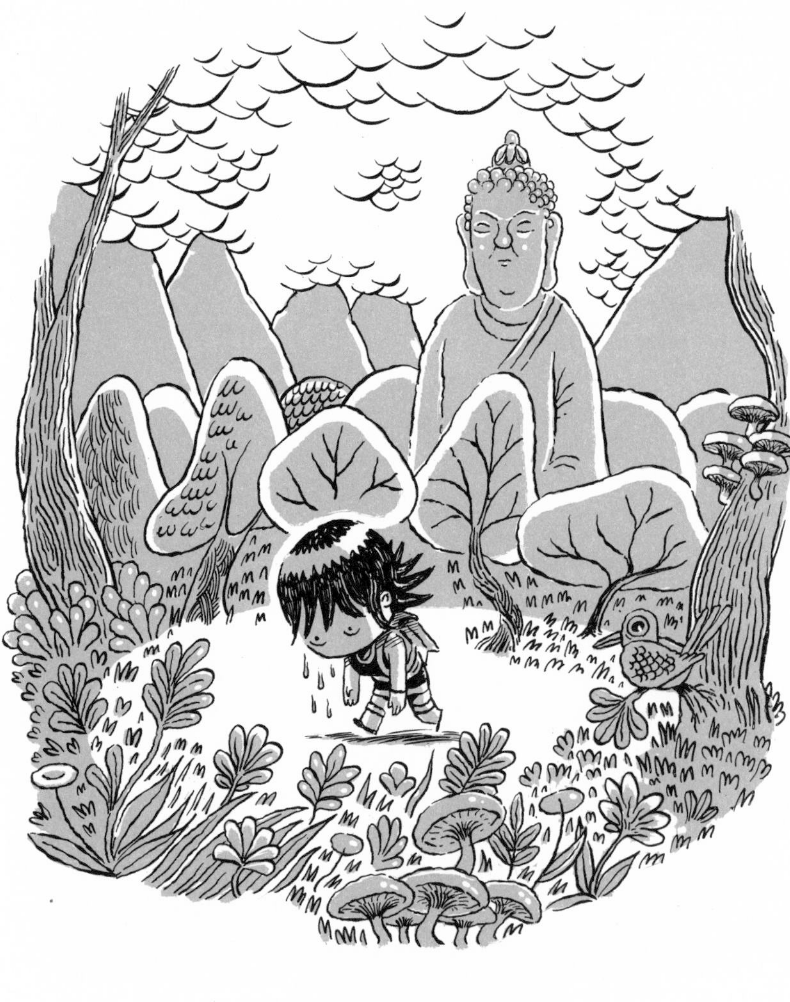

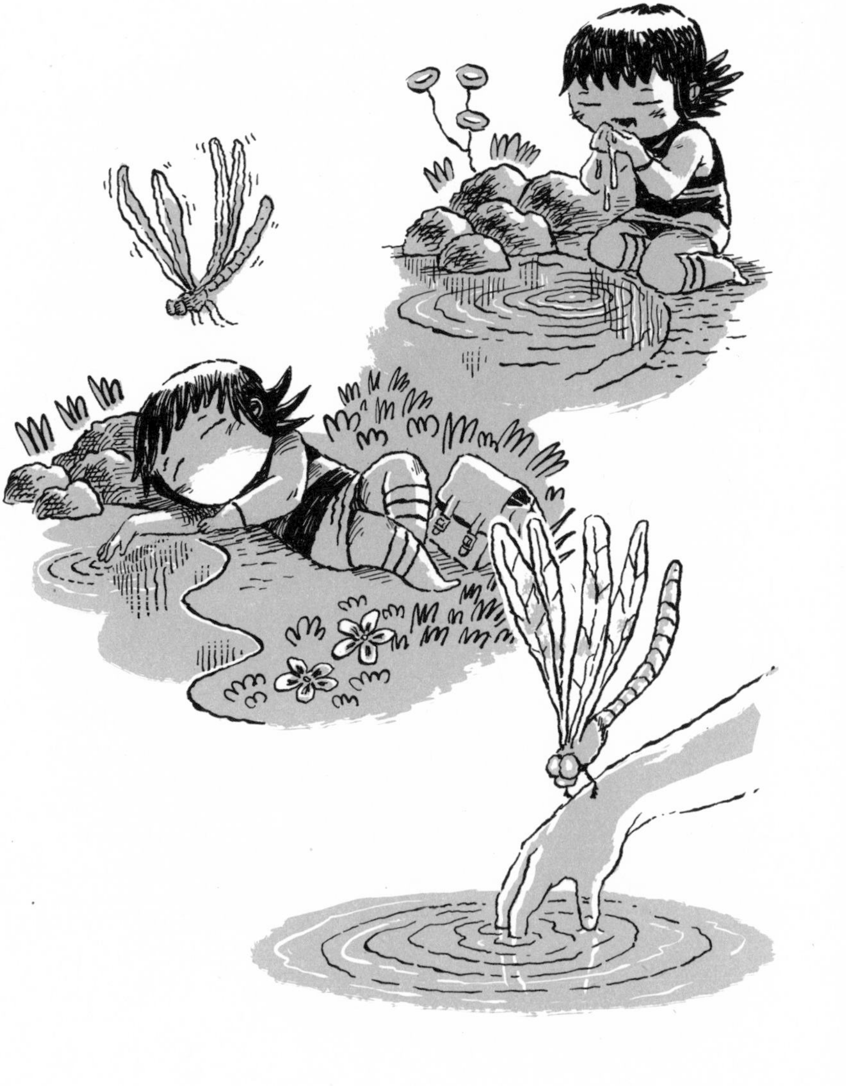

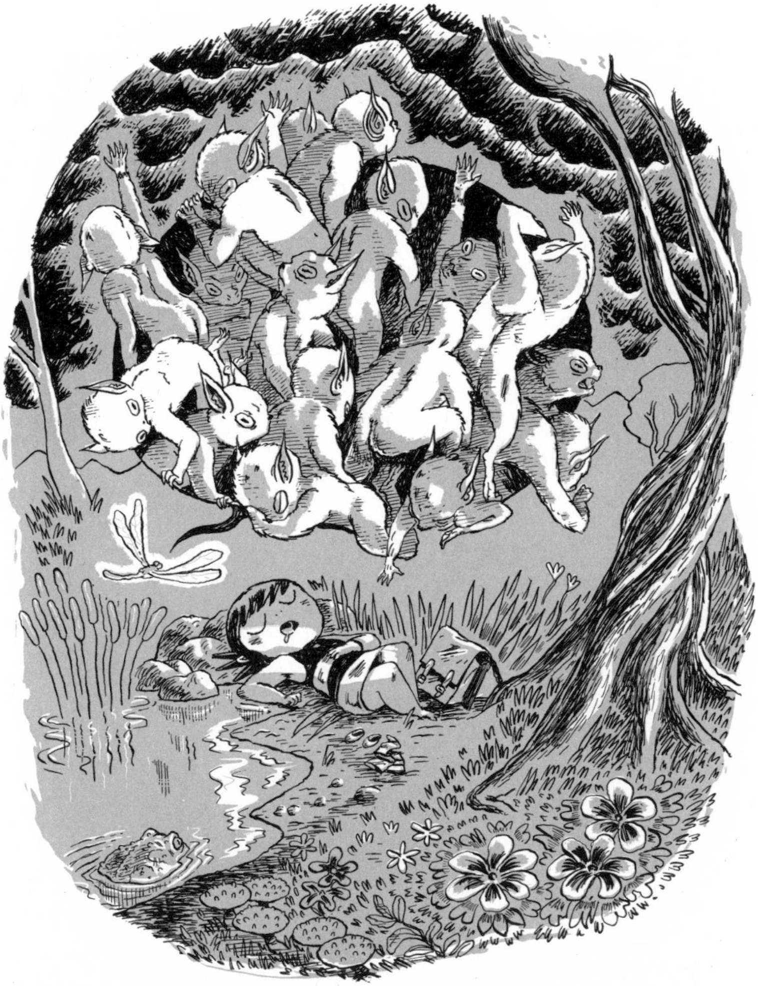

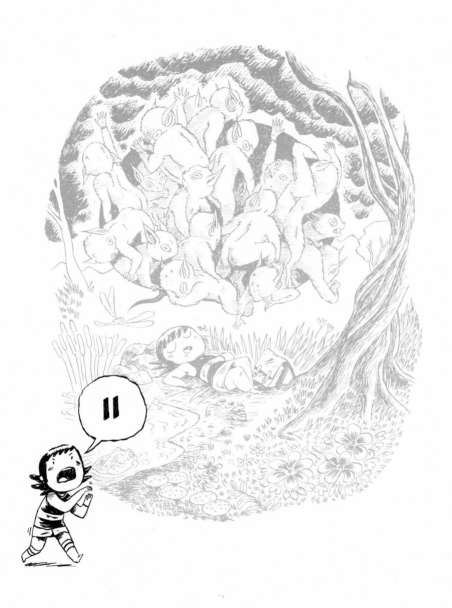

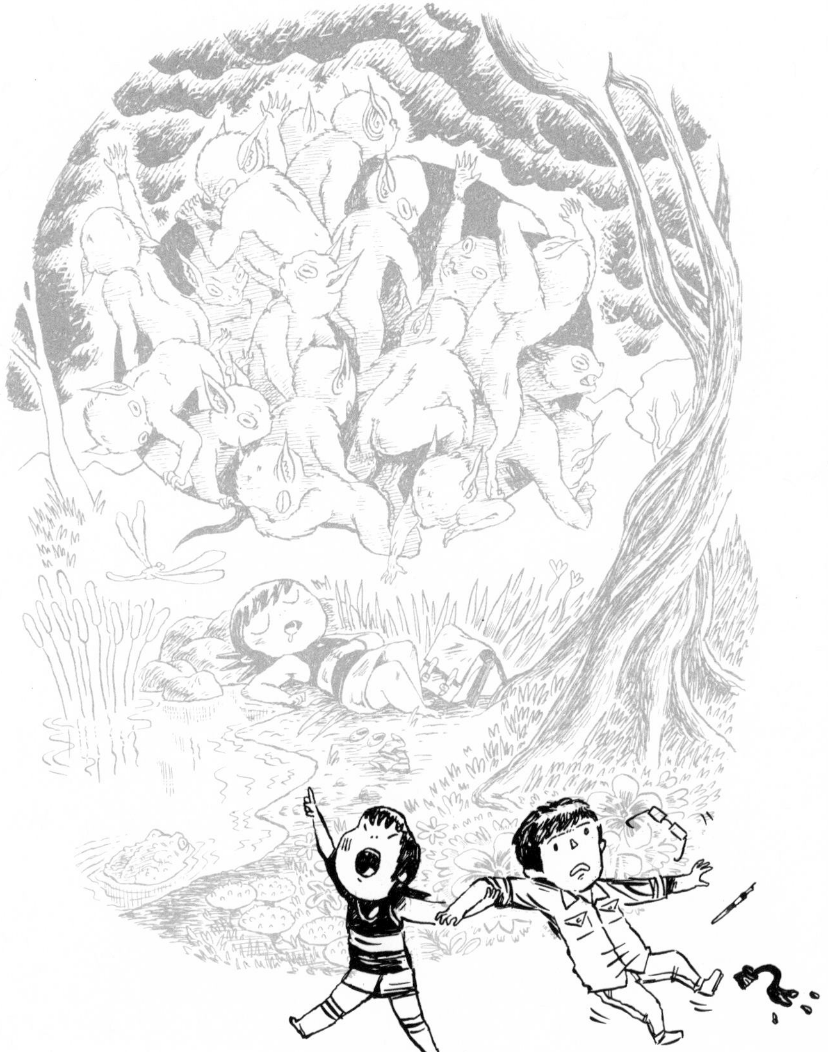

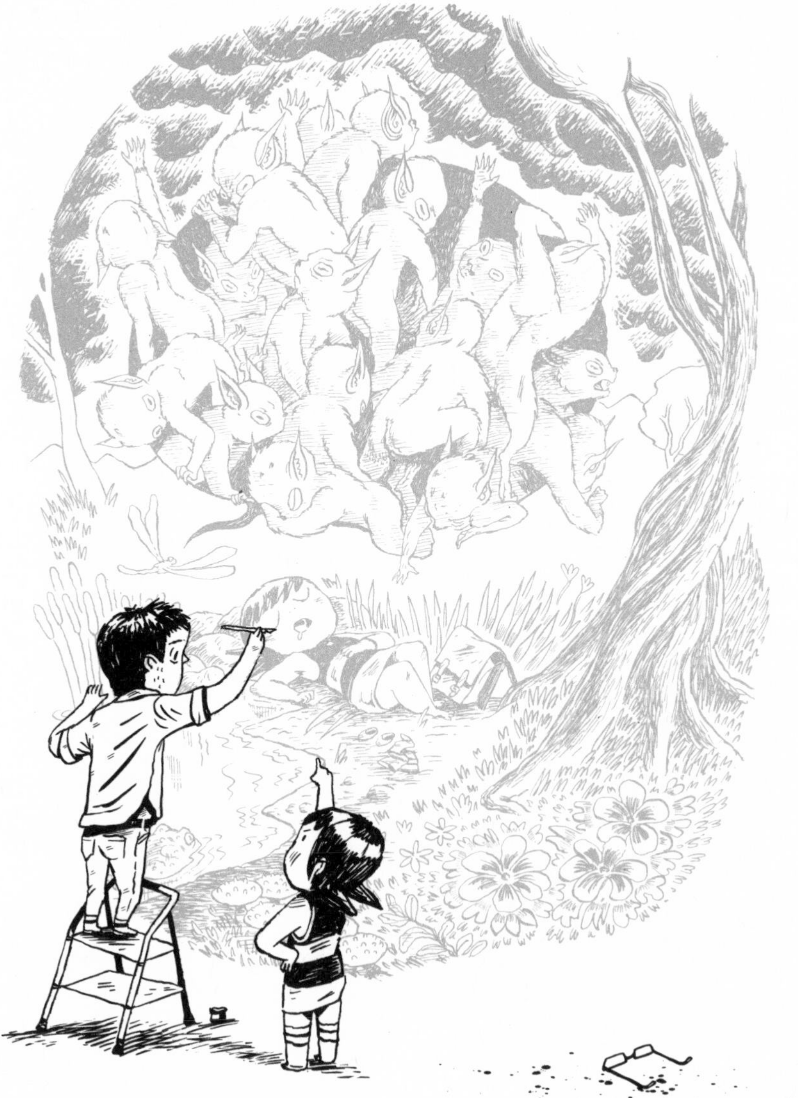

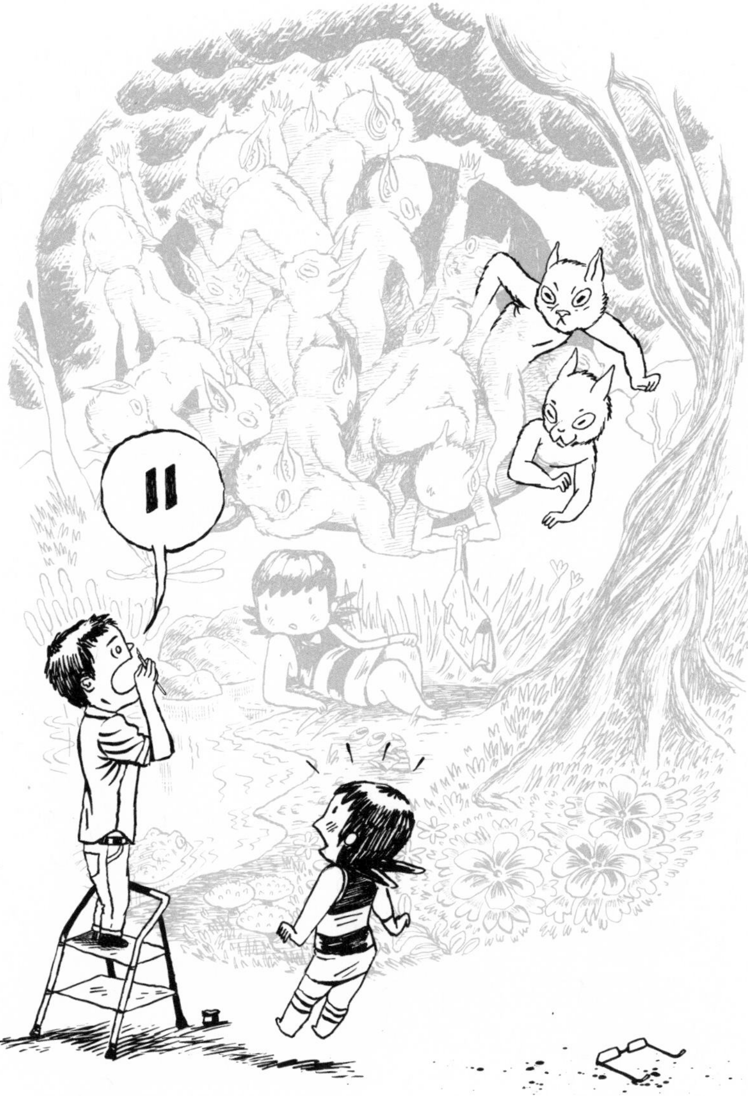

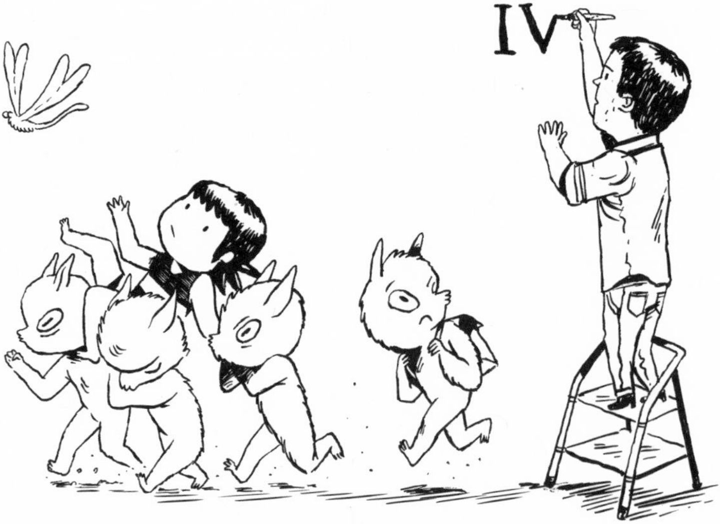
IV

IV.

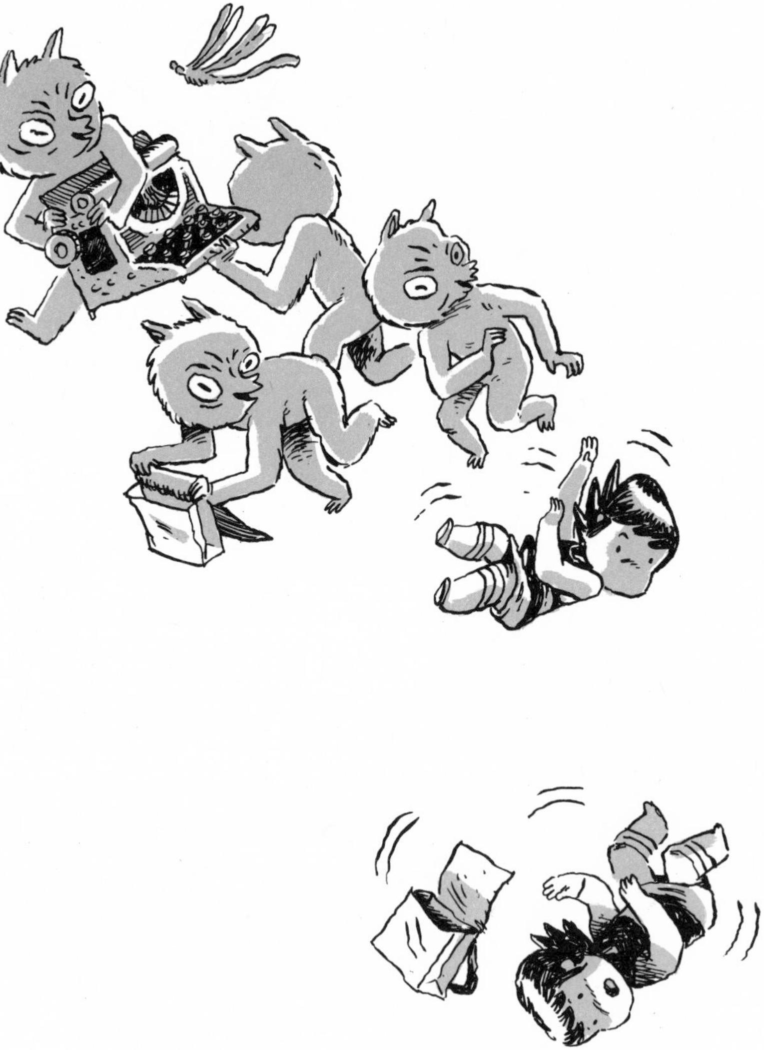

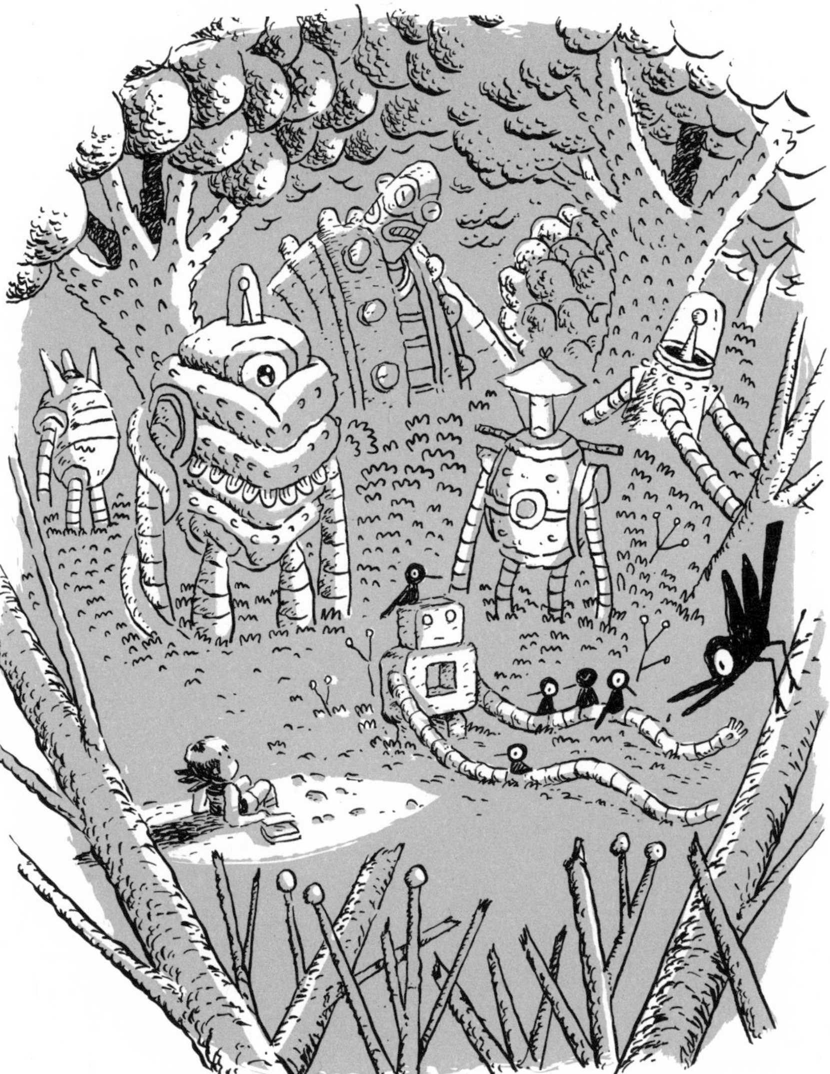

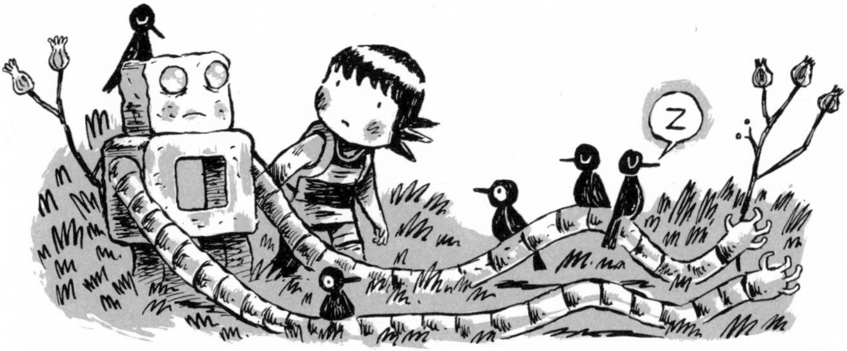
Z

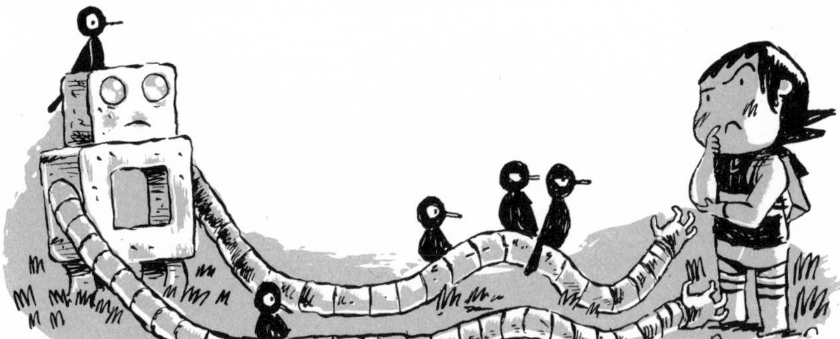

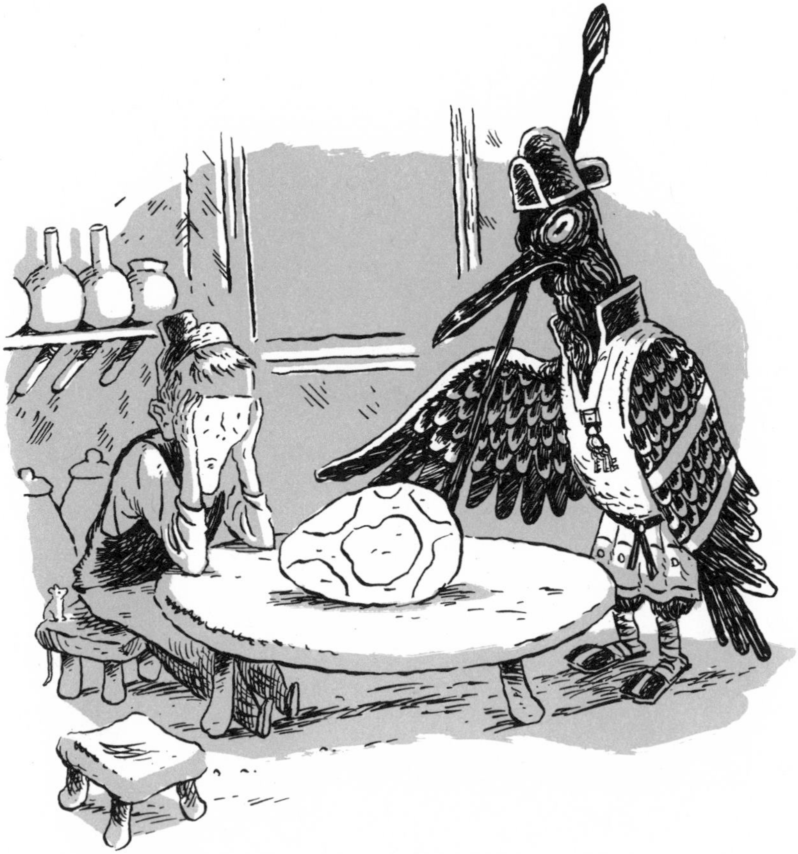

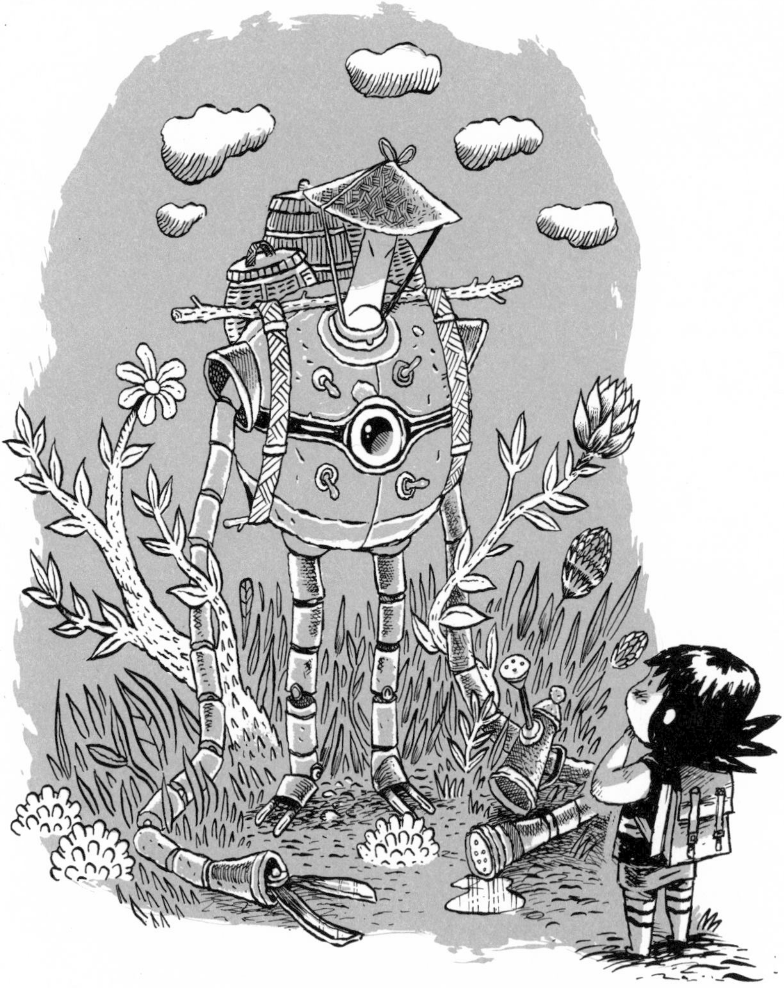

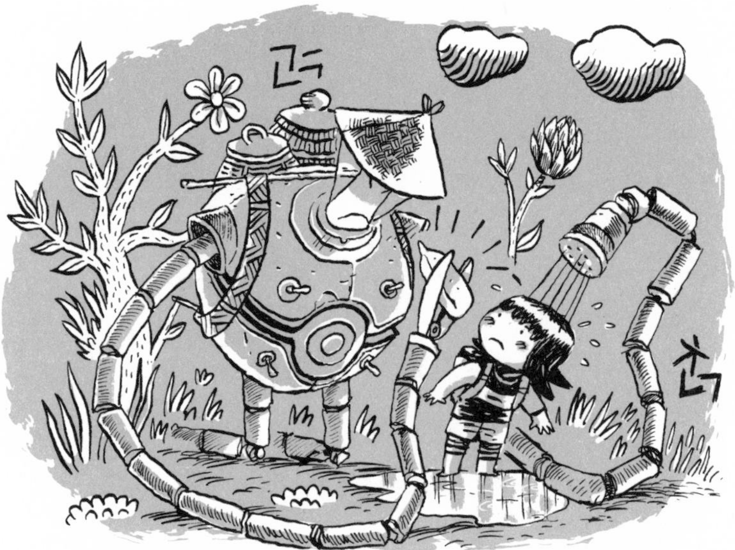

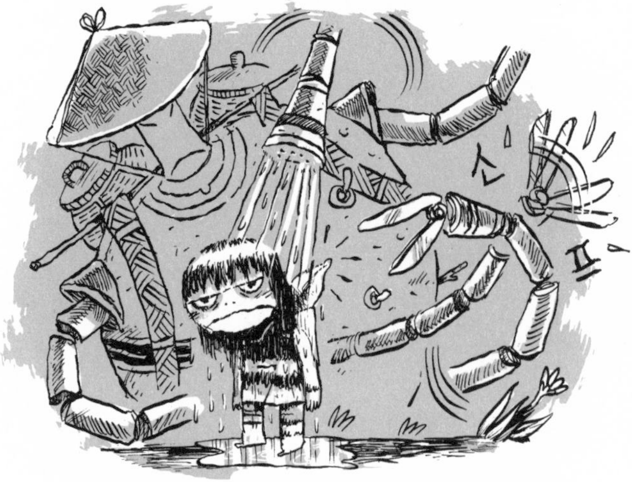

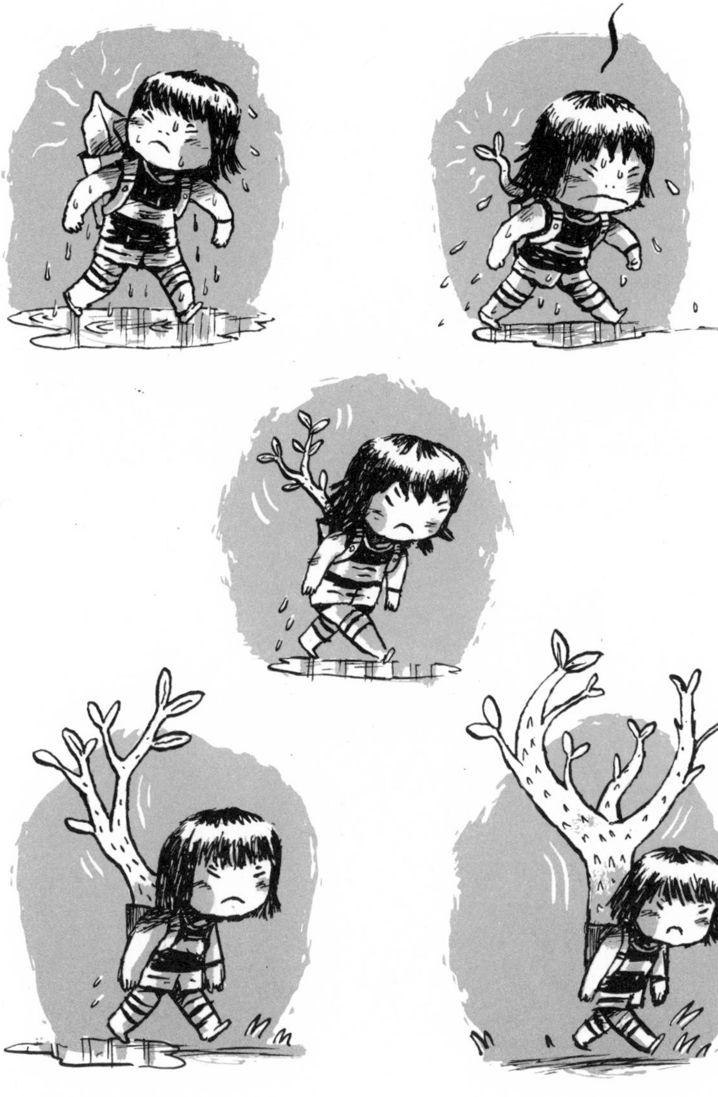

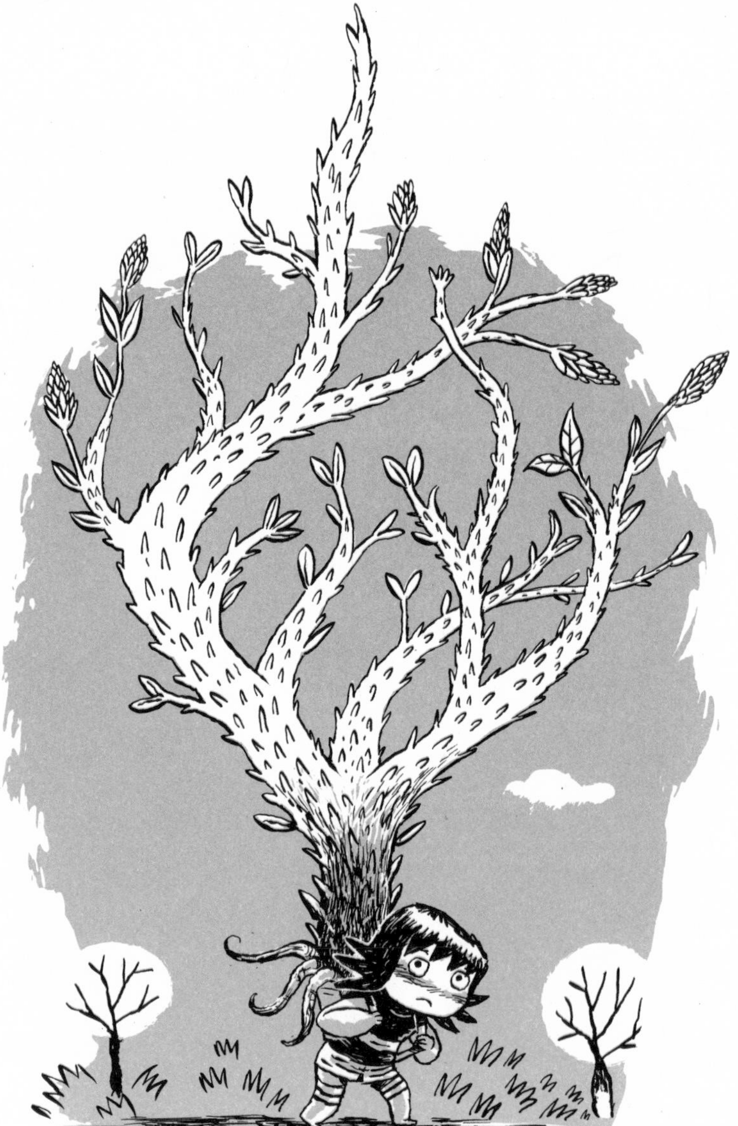

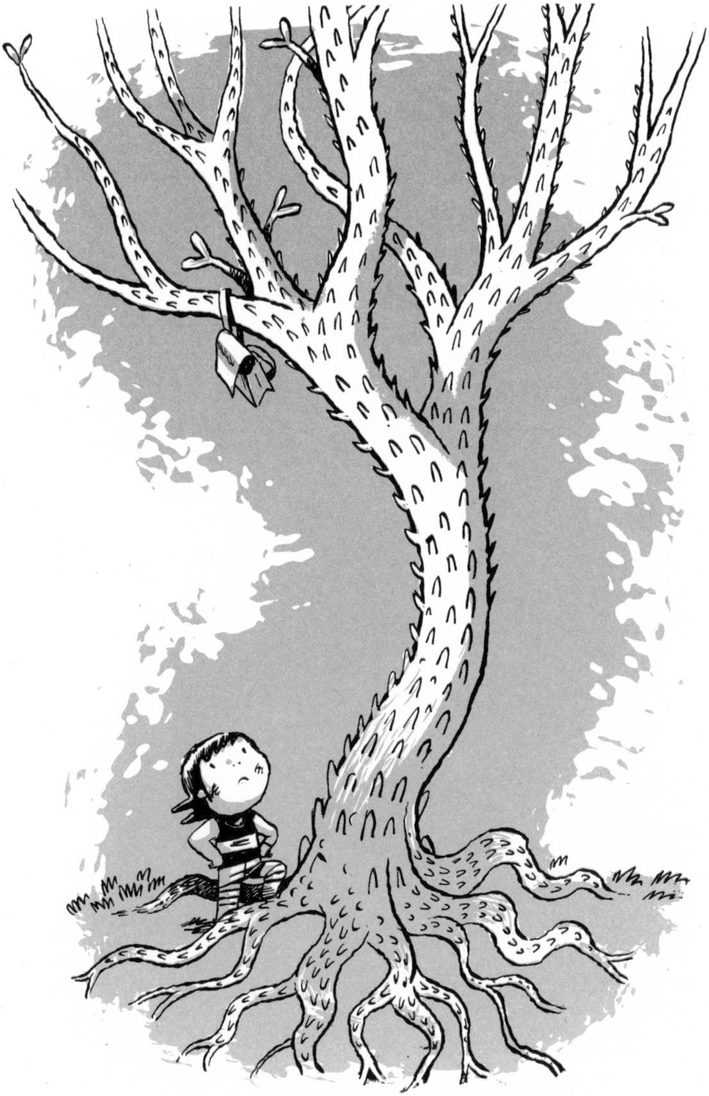

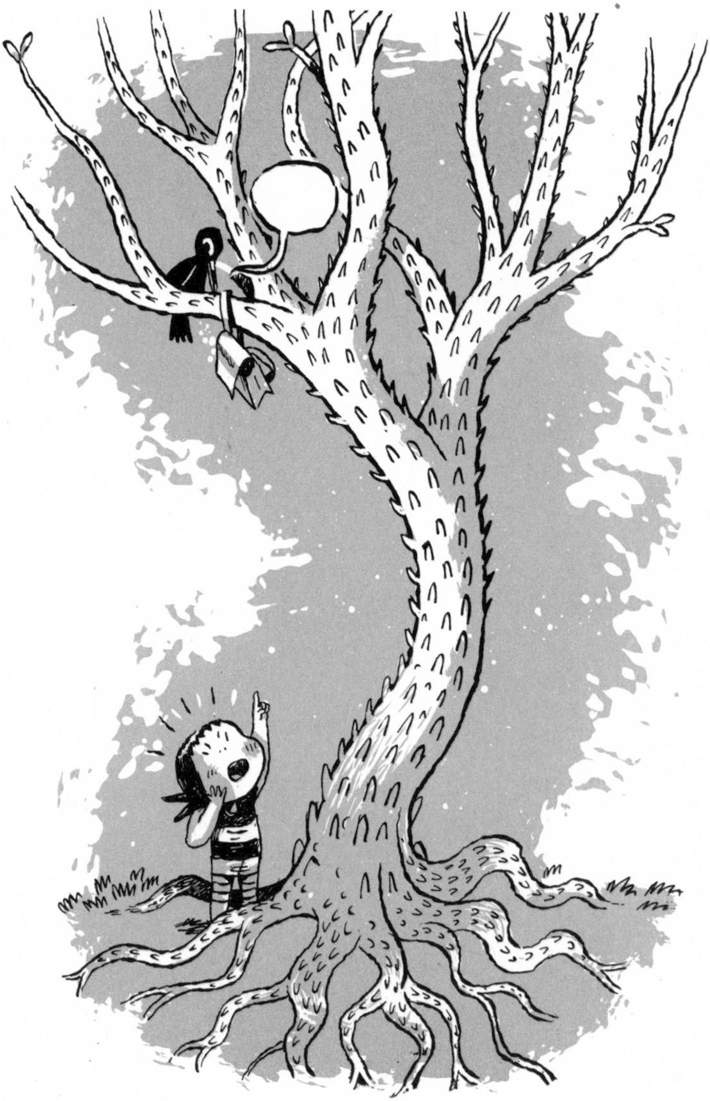

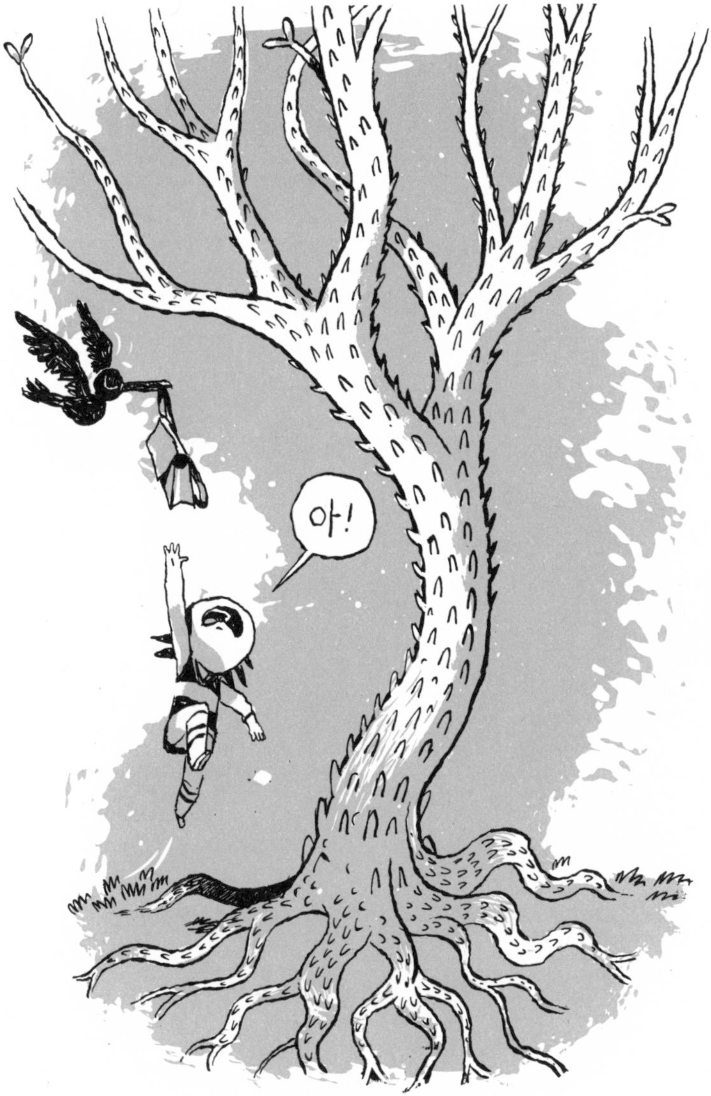
아!

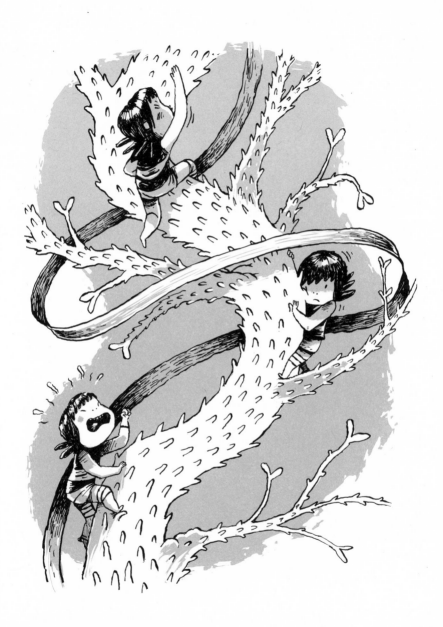

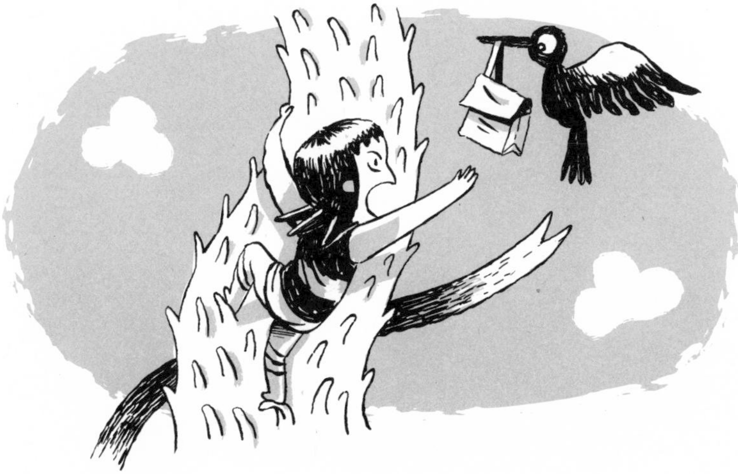

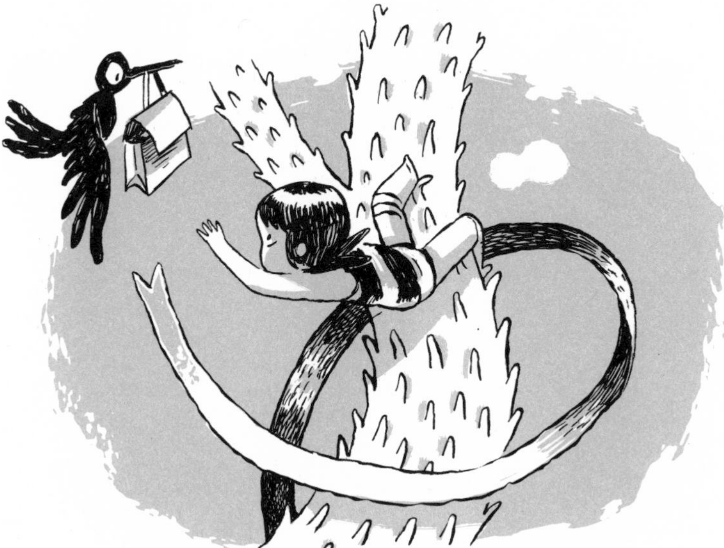

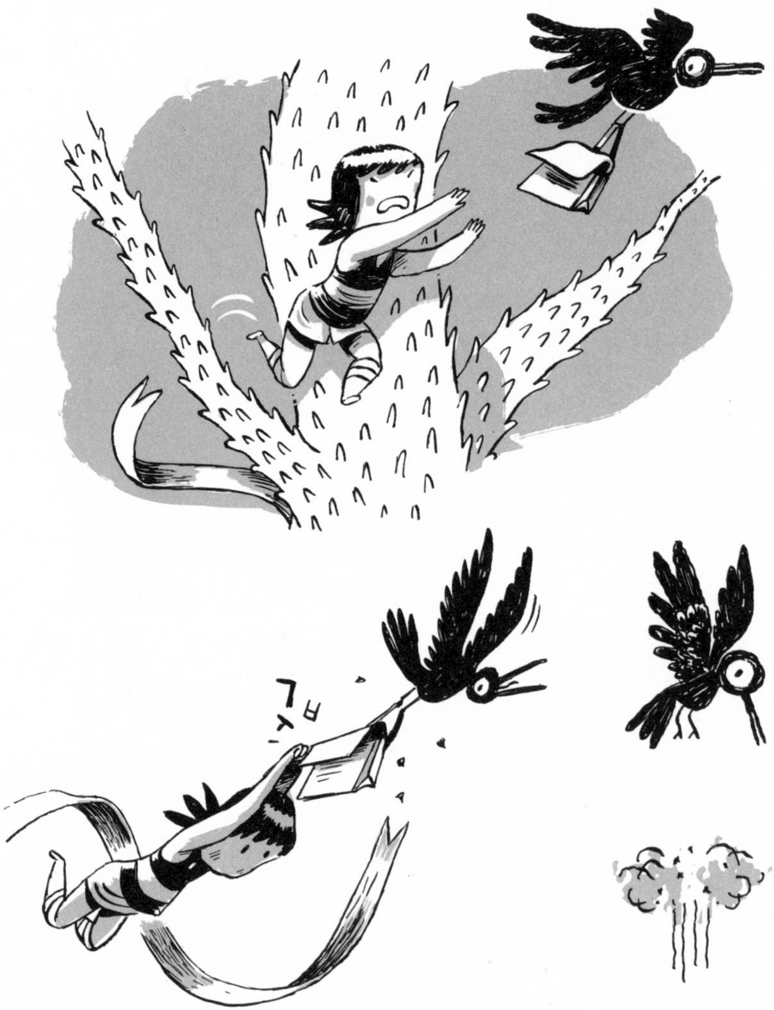

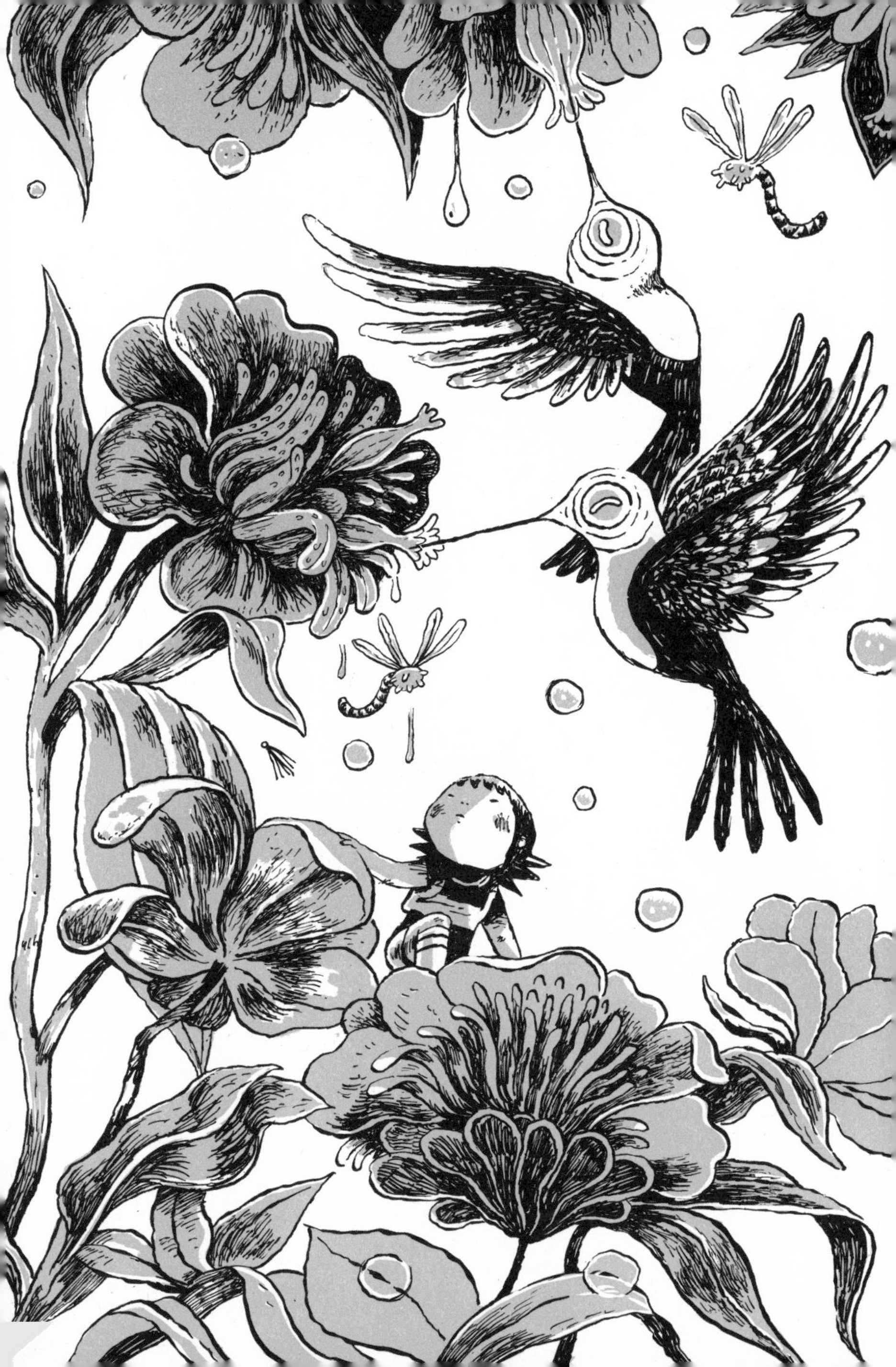

V.

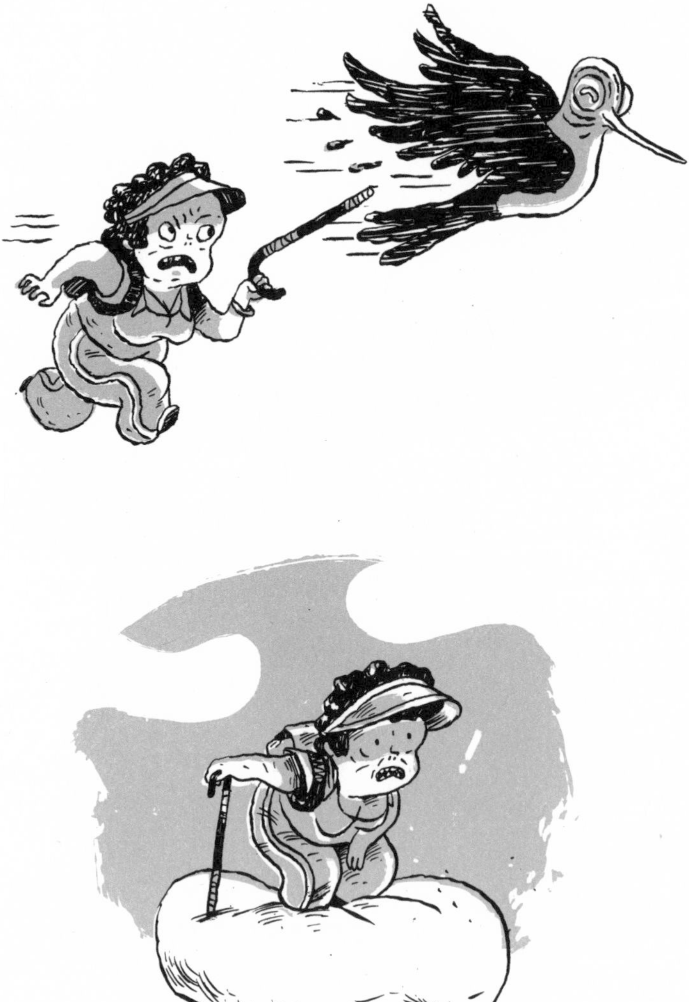

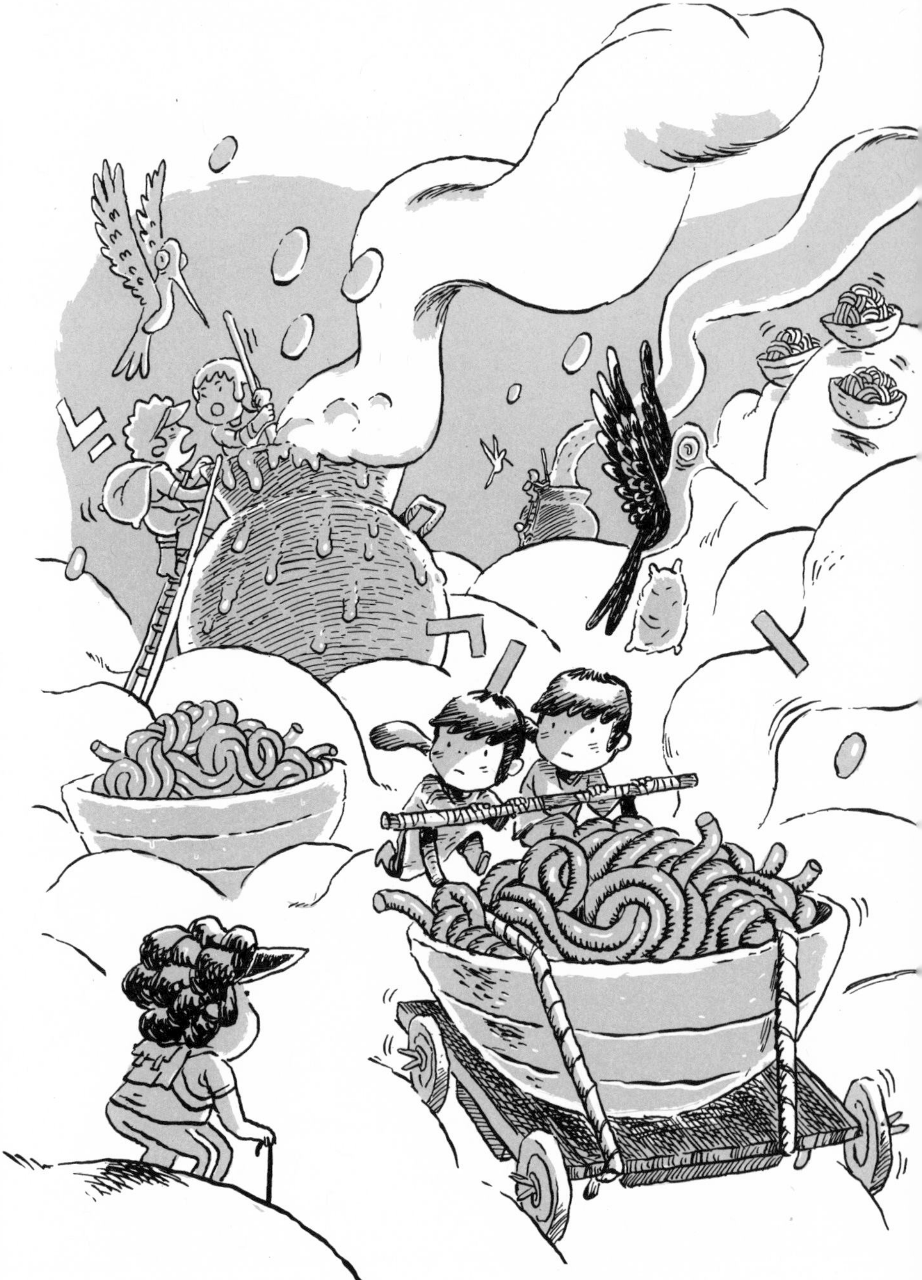

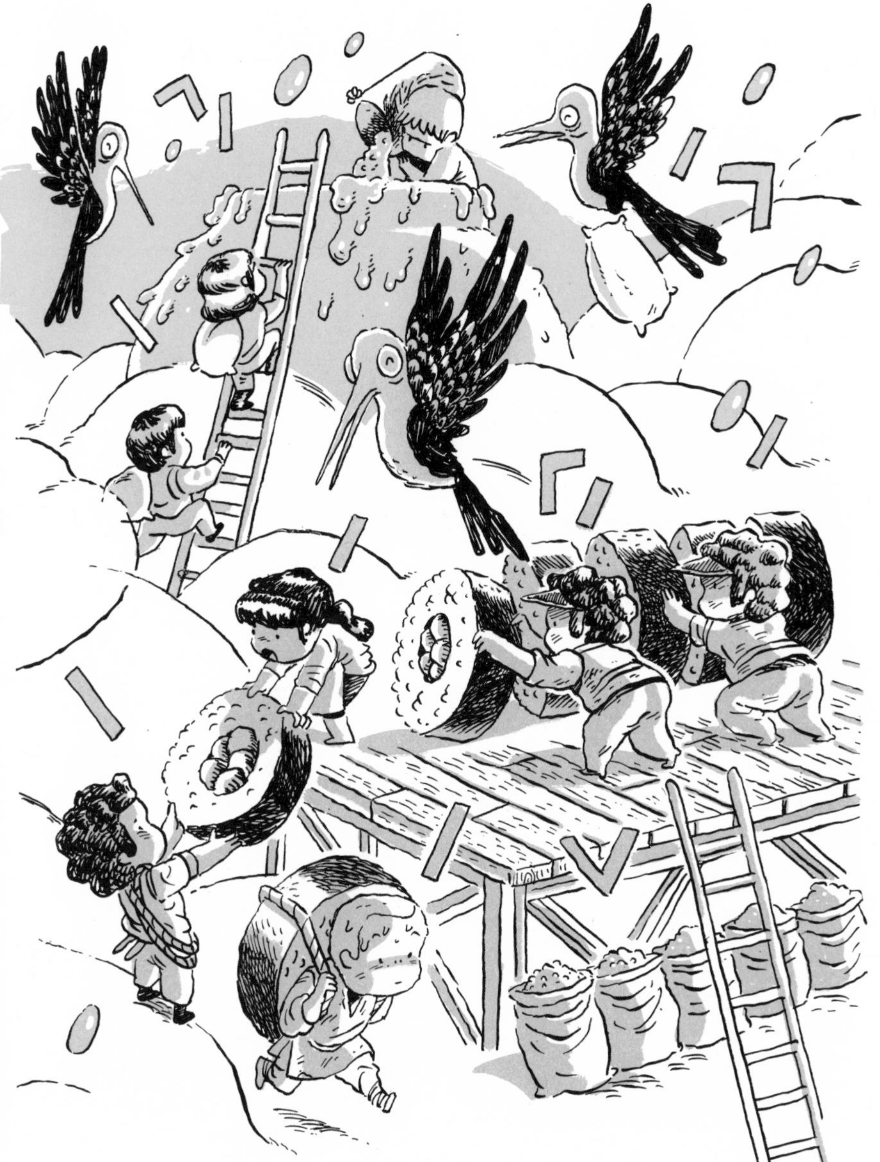

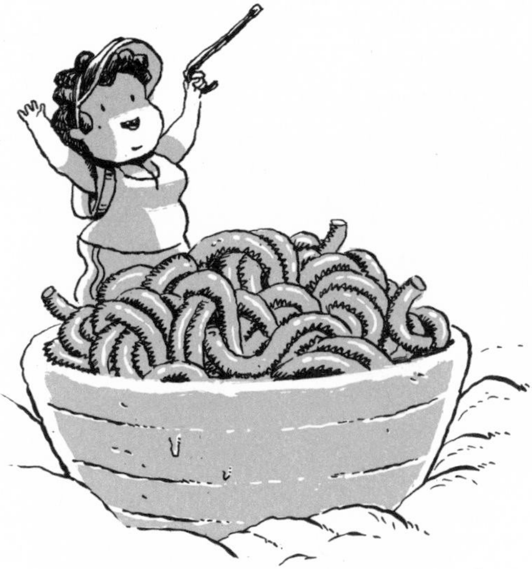

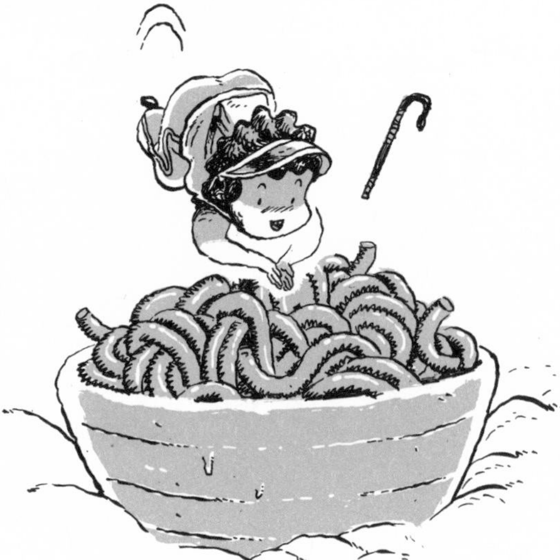

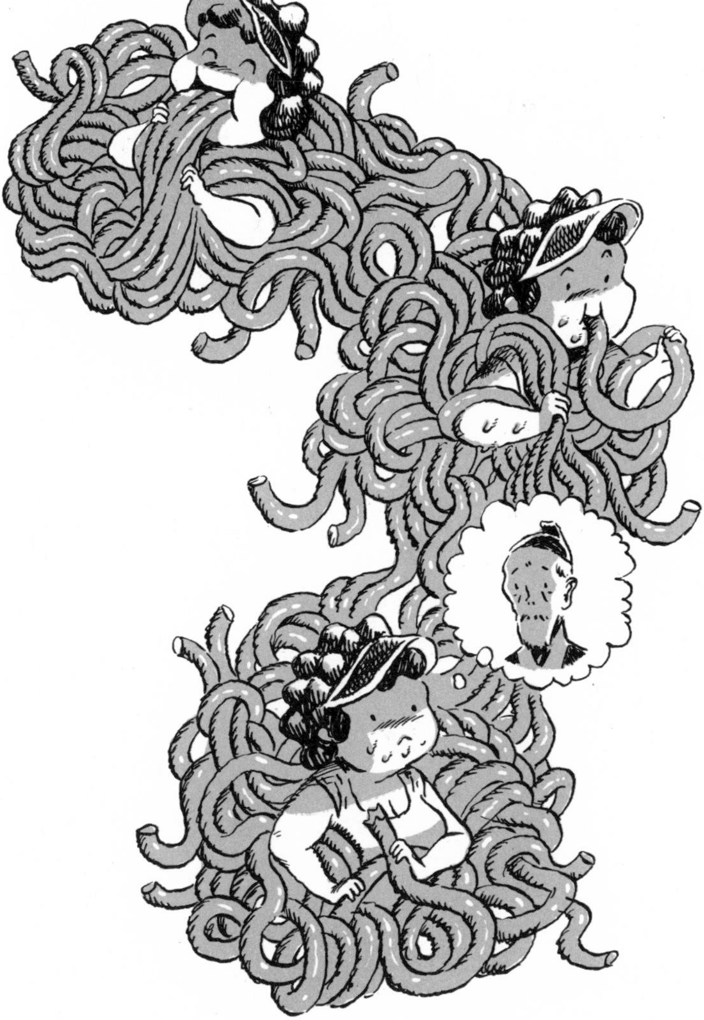

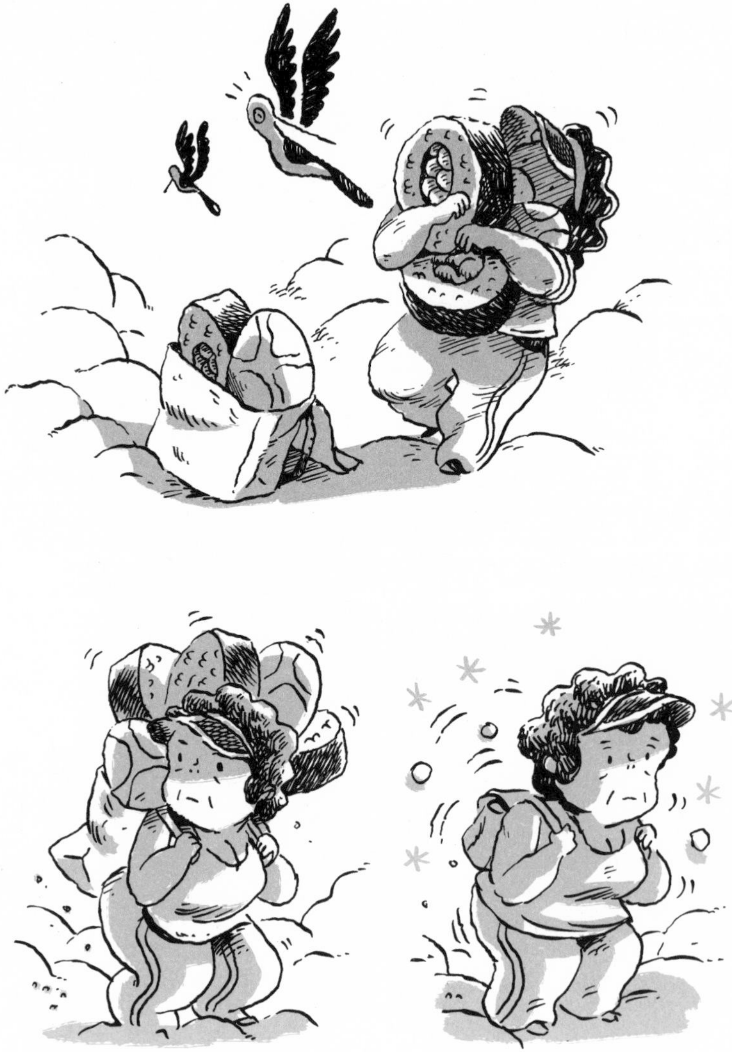

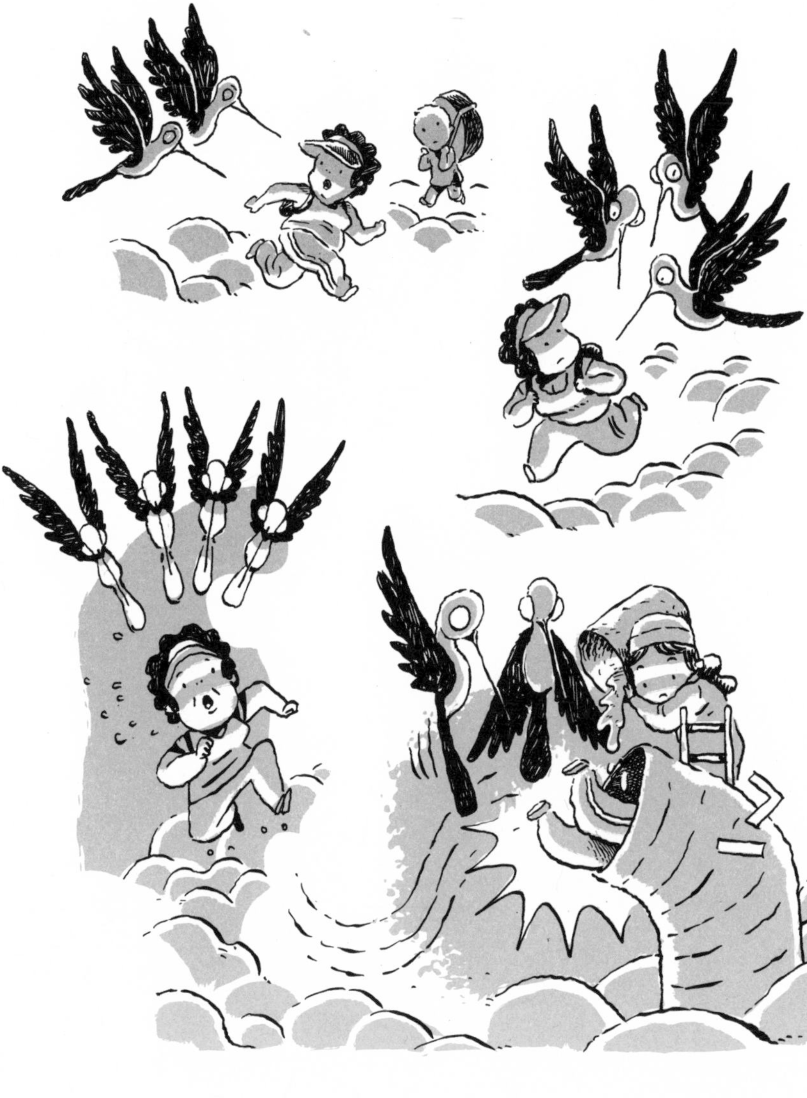

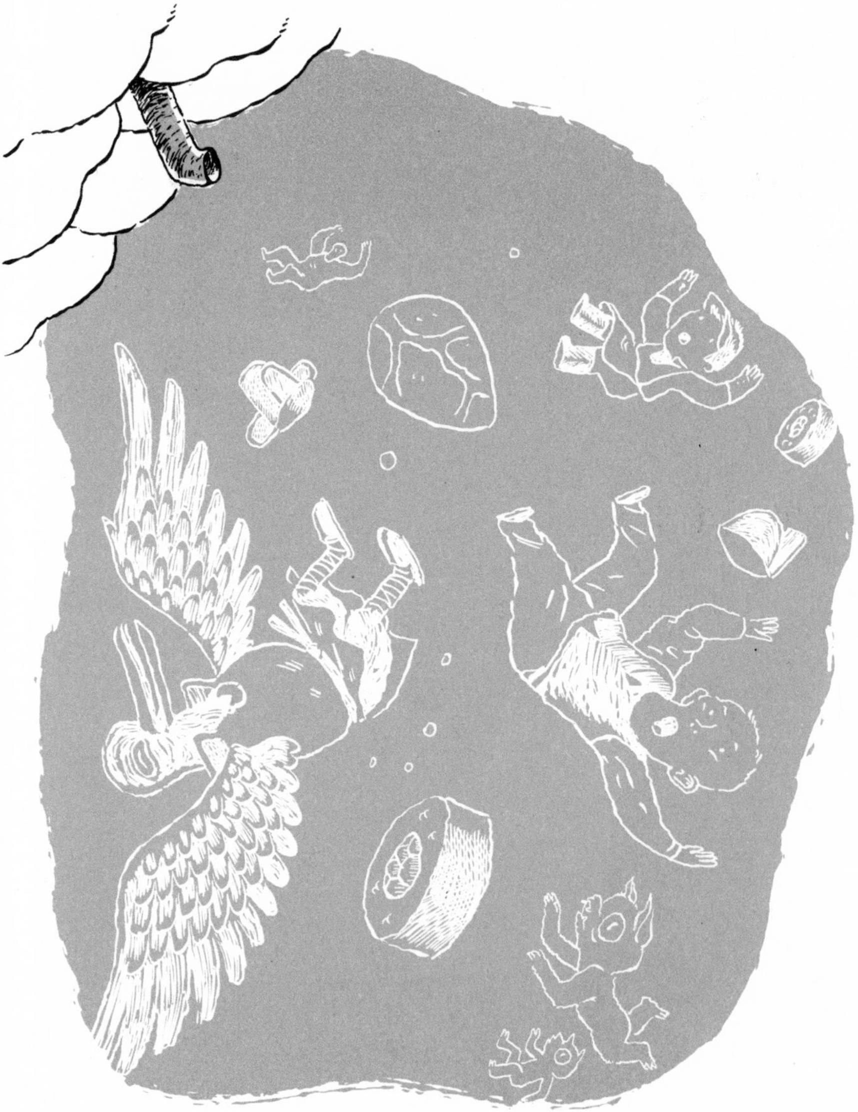

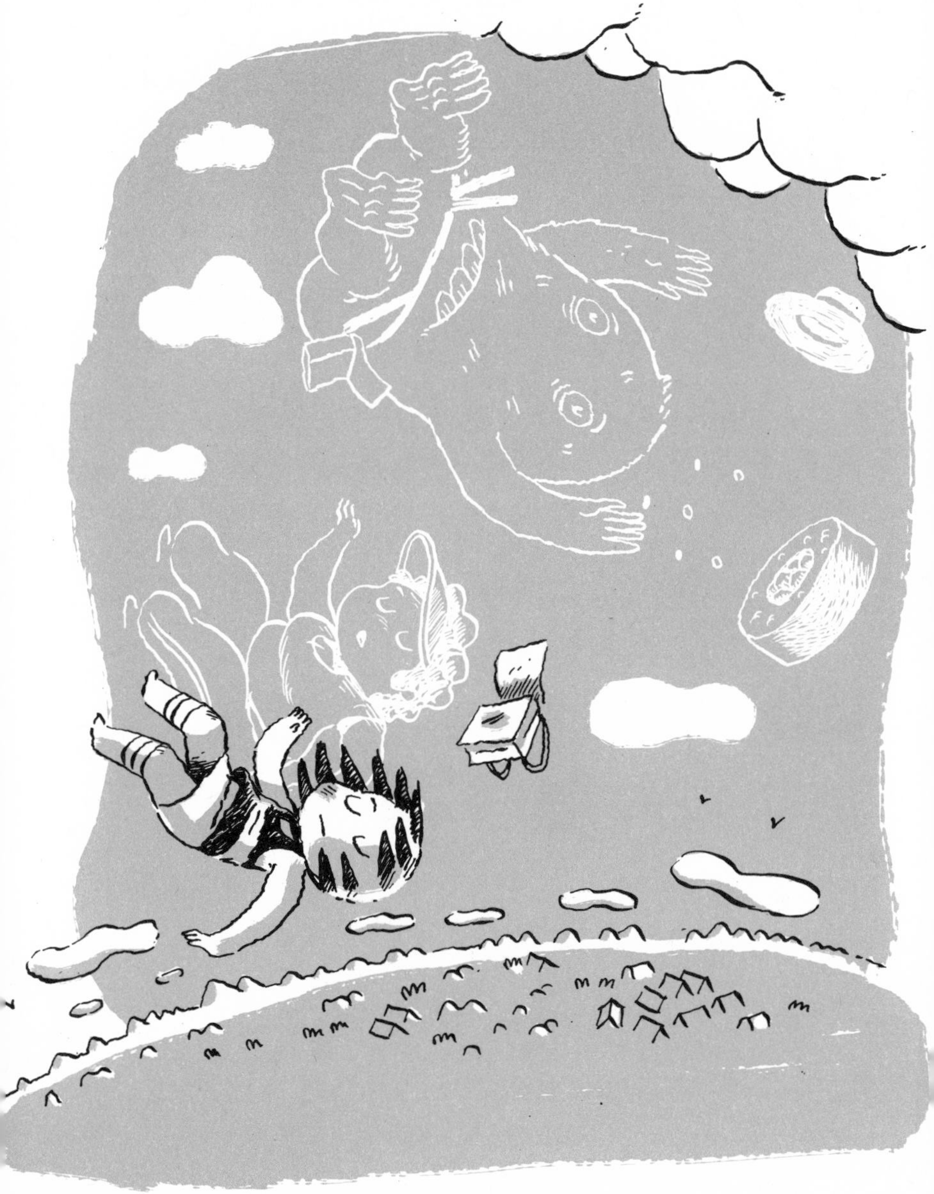

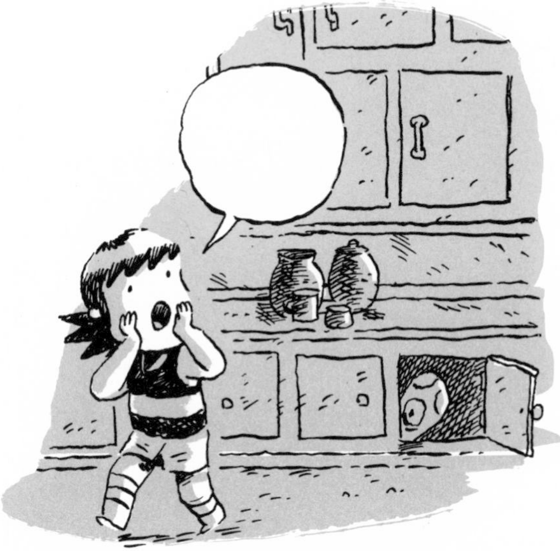

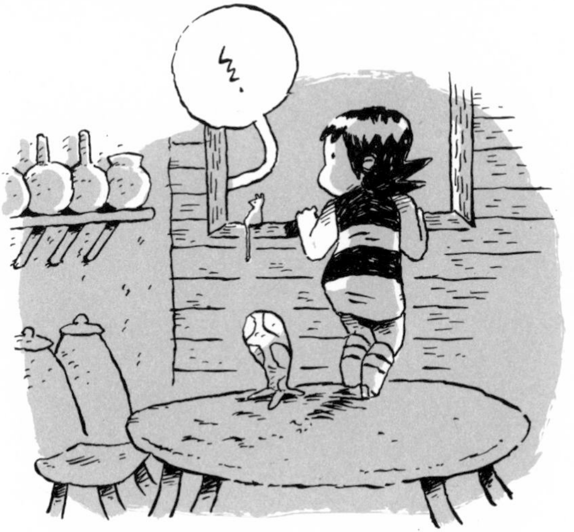

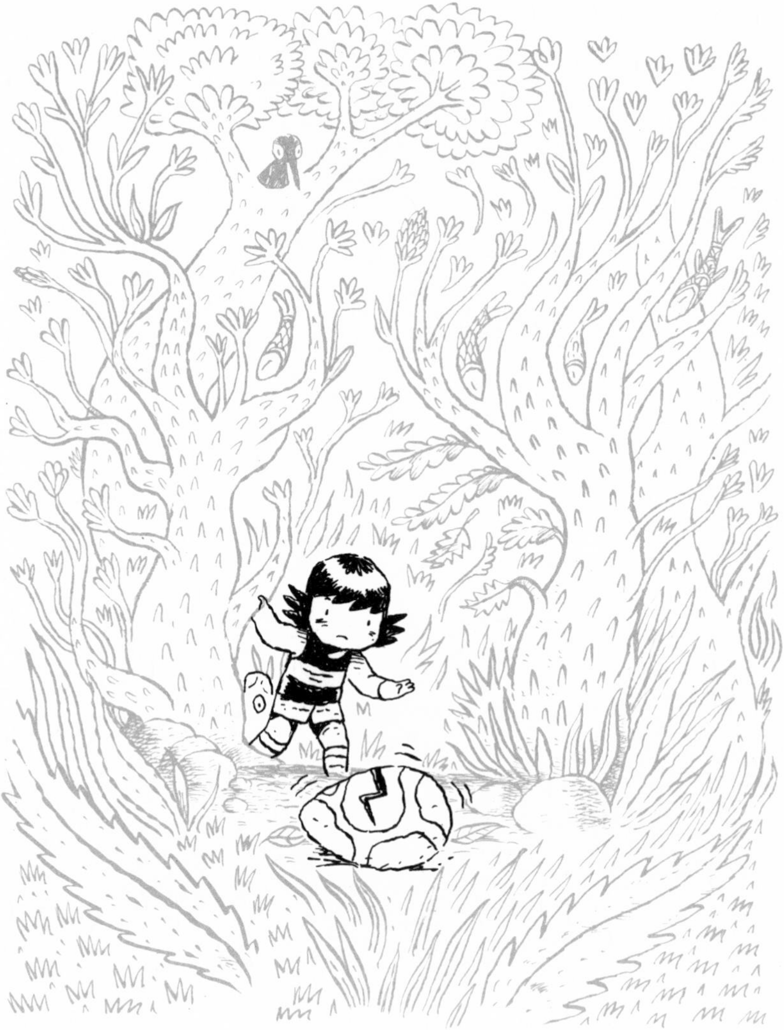

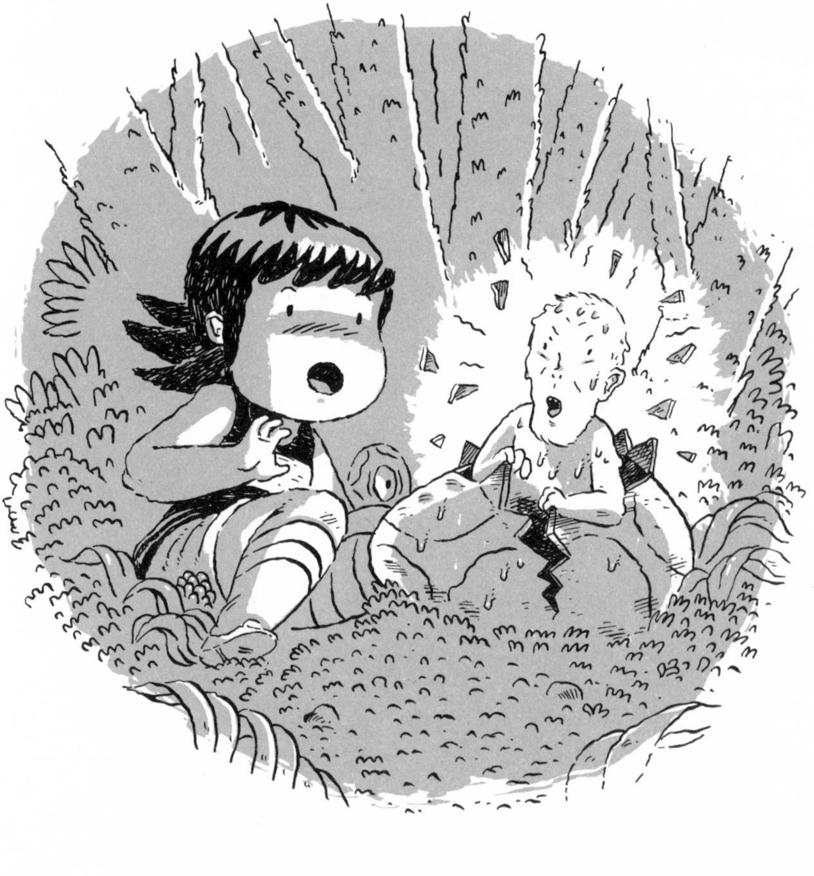

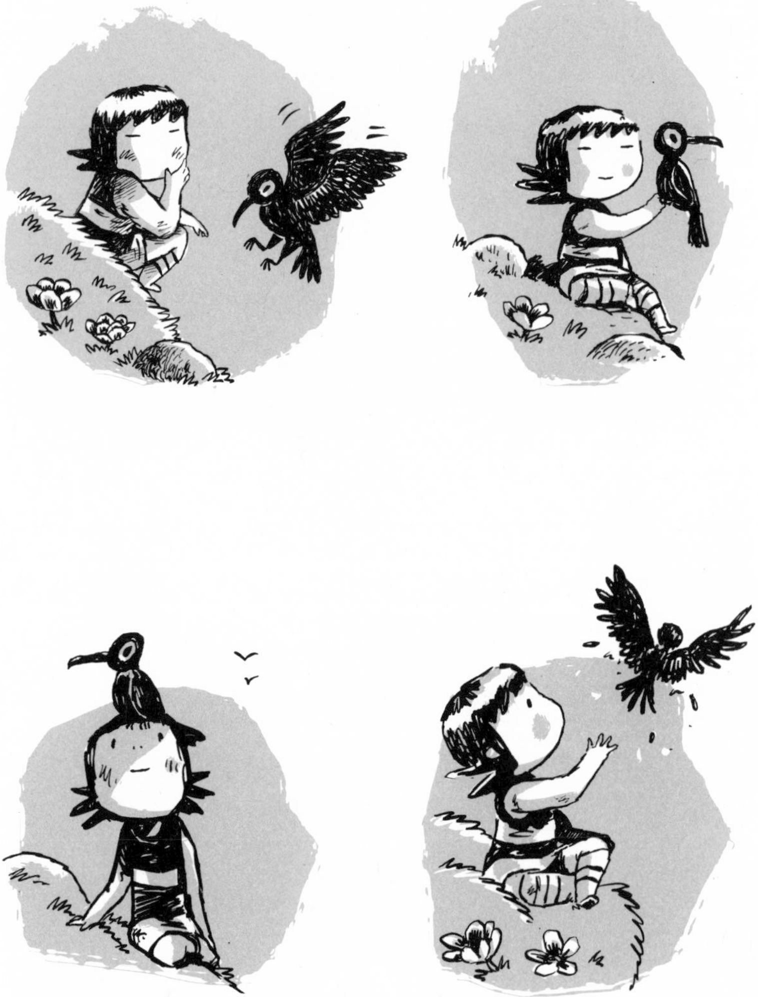

THANKS

aisling
chin-yee

james
braithwaite

hartley
lin

todd
wheatland

john martz

karl kerschl

brenden
fletcher

aaron
costain